D1128995

WELFARE
REFORMED

WELFARE REFORMED

A COMPASSIONATE APPROACH

Edited by David W. Hall

Richard J. Neuhaus   **R. C. Sproul, Jr.**
Doug Bandow   **George Grant**
Michael Bauman   **E. Calvin Beisner**
R. C. Sproul   **F. Edward Payne**

P & R PUBLISHING
Phillipsburg, New Jersey

LEGACY COMMUNICATIONS
Franklin, Tennessee

© 1994 by Legacy Communications. All rights reserved. Printed in
the United States of America.

Co-published April 1994 by Presbyterian & Reformed Publishing,
P.O. Box 817, Phillipsburg, NJ 08865-0817 and
Legacy Communications, P.O. Box 680365, Franklin, TN
37068-0365

No part of this publication may be reproduced, stored in a retrieval
system, or transmitted in any form by any means, electronic,
mechanical, photocopy, recording, or otherwise, without the prior
written permission of the publisher, except for brief quotations in
critical reviews or articles.

Chapter 4, "Statism: Land of the Free?": © Copyright 1993, *Table
Talk* magazine, Ligonier Ministries. Reprinted by permission.

Unless otherwise noted, all Scripture quotations are from the Holy
Bible, New International Version. © 1973, 1978, 1984 International
Bible Society. Used by permission of Zondervan Bible Publishers.

Library of Congress Cataloging-in-Publication Data

Welfare reformed : a compassionate approach / edited by David W. Hall.
    p. cm.
  Includes bibliographical references.
  ISBN 0-87552-301-3
  1. Public welfare—Religious aspects—Christianity. 2. Public
welfare—United States. 3. Church work with the poor—United
States. 4. Church and state—United States. 5. Welfare state.
6. Sociology, Christian—United States. 7. United States—Church
history—20th century. 8. United States—Social conditions—1980–
I. Hall David W., 1955–
8T738.48.W45   1994
261.8'32'0973—dc20   93-47039
                                                      CIP

CONTENTS

Foreword—Richard J. Neuhaus / *vii*

Introduction—David W. Hall / *1*

Part I—The Present State of the Welfare State: The Need for Reform

1. Toward a Post-statist Theological Analysis of Poverty—David W. Hall / *7*

2. Real Welfare Reform: An Idea Whose Time Has Come—Doug Bandow / *29*

3. What Went Wrong with Welfare: How Our Poverty Injured the Poor—Michael Bauman / *41*

4. Statism: Land of the Free?—R. C. Sproul and R. C. Sproul, Jr. / *55*

Part II—Welfare Reformed: Biblical Principles

5. Three Essential Elements of Biblical Charity: Faith, Family, and Work—George Grant / *67*

6. New Testament Developments: Principles into Action—David W. Hall / *85*

7. Poverty: A Problem in Need of Definition—E. Calvin Beisner / *111*

Part III—Another Reformation: Historical Models

8. Earlier Paradigms for Welfare Reform: The Reformation Period—David W. Hall / *133*

9. Against the Tide: Four Alternative Movements—George Grant / *165*

10. Welfare and Medical Care—F. Edward Payne, M. D. / *179*

11. A Non-Theological Postscript—David W. Hall / *191*

Appendix: The Oak Ridge Affirmations and Denials / *213*

Notes / *217*

Author Biographies / *229*

FOREWORD

Richard J. Neuhaus

In this foreword, Richard J. Neuhaus, dean of orthodox spokesmen on the interface of church and state matters in modern America, identifies one of the misperceptions of our day. Dr. Neuhaus, the Director of Religion and Public Life and Editor of First Things, *challenges the notion that the past generation of welfare has truly helped the poor, and questions whether present welfare practice is the most compassionate. Recognizing that most people do not have 'compassion fatigue', he sees the problem more accurately as a 'mendacity fatigue,' which can potentially erode the will to be compassionate. Welfare reform calls for a more comprehensive approach, targeting the whole person—not just economic subsidy.*

The First Step: Curing Caring, Fatigue

S ome will protest that the question posed by that title is outrageously wrongheaded. To ask what we should do about the poor, they say, smacks of paternalism and noblesse oblige, reflecting a hierarchical mentality in which the world is divided between "us" and "them." Rather, they would instruct us, we should speak of "standing in solidarity with the poor." The question is not what we should do for or about the poor; the question is whether we "identify" with the poor who are the victims of injustice perpetrated by those of us who are not poor. People who are given to such assertions simultaneously, and somewhat contradictorily, never relent in dramatizing the "needs" of the poor and berating the non-poor for their lack of "compassion." Pointing out needs, on the one hand, and the need to respond to such needs with compassion, on the other, does sound an awful lot like, well, charity. Which is fine since charity is but another word for love, and virtue does not come more golden than that.

Also from the other end of the political spectrum we are told that our question is wrong. There it is said that the real question is, What *can* we do about the poor? According to many conservatives, the answer is: little or nothing. It is pointed out that a bloated and bureaucratic welfare system, on which government at all levels is now spending an unprecedented billion per year, has only exacerbated the problems of poverty. Not only are more people classified as "poor" than ever before, but the underclass, composed largely of blacks and Hispanics, is locked into an intergenerational pattern of dependency that makes it almost certain that millions of people will never become self-supporting and law-abiding citizens.

That, in broad strokes, is the great divide in public discussions of what is to be done about domestic poverty. The divide generally follows the lines of what are described as liberal and conservative dispositions. The liberals are today at a distinct disadvantage in the discussion and increasingly recognize that they are on the defensive. The equation between compassion and increased government expenditure is increasingly unpersuasive. Despite complaints about cutbacks during the Reagan and Bush years, welfare budgets have in fact grown and grown during the same time that—and this by liberal accounts—poverty has gotten worse and worse. It now seems obvious to most Americans that "throwing money" at the problem of poverty is not the answer.

We hear a great deal about how Americans are suffering from compassion fatigue. That is why, we are told, Democratic politicians are pitching to the middle class and avoiding the party's traditional themes of helping the disadvantaged. On the left of the party—that is, to the extreme left of the political mainstream of which the national party has in recent decades been the far left—such politicians are accused of selling out the principles of liberalism. The more likely explanation is that some Democrats have decided to win a few policy arguments for a change, and they recognize that the middle class is where the votes are, since most Americans (including many who are designated as poor) think of themselves as middle class. In addition, some Democrats have come to share the near-universal perception that measuring compassion by the appropriation of tax dollars is a truly dumb idea whose time came and went long ago. On questions of domestic poverty, resistance to liberal bromides may be an indicator not of diminished caring but of increased understanding. Americans are suffering not from compassion fatigue but from what might be termed mendacity fatigue.

Americans more and more realize that they have, over many years, been lied to about poverty, and they don't like it one bit. They have had enough and they are not going to take it anymore. In the last thirty years, literally trillions of tax dollars have been spent on "helping the poor," with the result, they are told, that there are more poor people than ever and they are worse off than ever. Not only that: crime is running amok, abortion and out-of-wedlock births skyrocket, parasitic urban males are permanently at war with the culture by age fifteen, and city school systems seem incapable of delivering anything but multicultural trashings of societal values and condoms. Meanwhile, those who are aptly called the povertycrats in charge of this human shambles demand billions of dollars more in the name of compassion. It is little wonder that, in our political vocabulary, compassion is becoming a dirty word. When voters hear a politician mention compassion, they reach for their pocket books—not to give but to make sure they are still there.

Perennial alarms are raised about the dangers of a popular backlash against the poor, and against poor blacks in particular. Those who sound that tocsin usually accompany it with the demand that more money be devoted to poverty—the bulk of it for the expansion of the bureaucracies of the poverty industry, with just enough going to poor people to keep them in the agitated discontent to which they have become accustomed, destroying their neighborhoods rather than ours. While warnings about a backlash have typically been exaggerated, the time has come to take such warnings more seriously. In the absence of greater candor and of more credible remedies, many Americans are fed up with the question of poverty, and therefore fed up with hearing about poor people. At least they are fed up with hearing about them from politicians, and may be in a mood to give a hearing to very different politicians who tell them that they are right to be indifferent, or worse, to the poor. The prospect that this mood might spread is fraught with ugliness, and not least racial ugliness.

Popular fatigue is intensified by recklessly inflated statements about the dimensions of poverty in America. Sensible people refrain from taking on unmanageable problems. Although they do not quite put it that way, the message of the povertycrats is that the problem of poverty is unmanageable. What else are people to make of the claim that during a decade of stunning prosperity (despite the recent recession) there was an alarming increase in the number of Americans classified as poor? One thing people might make of it is to more closely examine the claim. That is precisely what is done in a number of recent studies.

According to the Census Bureau, over thirty million Americans are living in poverty. That figure is larger than in the 1960s when the war on poverty was launched, and this despite the fact that welfare spending, adjusting for inflation, rose throughout the 1970s and 1980s to its present all-time high. The official poverty line is a cash income of $12,675 annually for a family of four or $10,419 for a family of three. Those below that line are classified as poor. But who are these "poor" people? The appeal for compassion is accompanied by images of people living in cardboard boxes, of children with hunger-distended bellies, bony ribs, and sunken eyes in this, the land of plenty. There are such people, to be sure. Too many of them. But nowhere near thirty million or even three million of them.

Consider but a few items. Thirty-eight percent of persons classified as poor own their own homes. The median value of these homes is $39,200, or 58 percent of the median value of all homes owned by Americans. Nearly half a million "poor" persons own homes worth over $100,000, and 36,000 "poor" persons own homes worth over $300,000. Sixty-two percent of "poor" households own a car, and 14 percent own two or more cars. Nearly half of all "poor" households have air conditioning, and 31 percent have microwave ovens. Poor people, on average, consume the same level of vitamins, minerals, and protein as do middle-class folk, and poor children actually eat more meat and protein than do their middle-class peers. Poor adults are more likely to be overweight than those in the middle class.

Keep in mind that poverty is defined by reported cash income. That does not include income from what is politely called the informal economy. Moreover, the government's own data show that low-income households spend $1.94 for every one dollar of income reported. That is because the official poverty definition does not include non-cash, in-kind assistance such as food stamps, housing subsides, and Medicaid. If all welfare benefits are included, the government is spending over $11,120 on every "poor" family in America. The claim that there are more than thirty million Americans "living in poverty" only intensifies the distrust that is corrupting our public life and distracting attention from the very real problem of poverty in this country.

Numerous government reports make clear that most "poor" Americans today are better housed, better fed, and own more personal property than average U.S. citizens throughout most of this century. After adjusting for inflation, the per capita expenditures of the lowest-income one-fifth of the U.S. population today exceed the per capita income of the median American household in 1955. The average "poor" American lives in a larger house or apartment, eats far more meat, and is more likely to have a car and dishwasher than is the average West European. Such "poor" people are poor in the sense that they are less affluent than other Americans, but they are not poor in any way that constitutes a national crisis or occasions moral outrage. And, of course, most poor people do not remain poor. If we accept the government definition of poverty and make the appropriate adjustments for inflation, the majority of Americans over forty years old today once "lived in poverty." The great majority of Americans do not believe that, which is one reason for mendacity fatigue.

Chicago Tribune columnist Mike Royko has been looking at the data and he reports this exchange with a fictional barroom interlocutor who is not impressed by all the talk about rampant poverty in America:

> "You are as lacking in compassion as those awful conservatives."

> "No, I ain't. Just the opposite. This stuff about all the millions of poor people makes me proud to be an American."

> "You are proud that we have millions of poor in this country? How revolting."

"No, look at it this way. If I had told my old man: 'Pa, when I grow up, I'm gonna have a little house, one or two cars, air conditioning, a space-age microwave oven, a TV, and spend two bucks for every buck that comes in,' he would have said: 'Only in America.'"

"Yes, but what would he have said if you told him that despite these possessions, you were still classified as poor?"

"He would have said: 'Go for it, kid.'"

Of course Mr. Royko is being frightfully incorrect. We all know that poverty is no laughing matter. It really is not, once we cut through the mendacity and get to the real crisis of poverty in America. The real crisis is related less to income than to behavior, less to economics than to culture. The real crisis is the underclass, a mainly urban and still growing population of those who are "radically isolated" (William Julius Wilson) from the mainstream of American patterns of opportunity and responsibility. For them, the status quo of the welfare system is much more the problem than the solution. Not only the work habits but the most elementary patterns of family and child-rearing have been debased to the point of destruction.

In the 1950s, nearly one-third of poor families were headed by adults who worked full time throughout the year. That figure today is 16 percent. Even using the Census Bureau's skewed definition of poverty, only 5.6 percent of married-couple families are today "living in poverty." In 1959, 28 percent of poor families with children were headed by women. Today, over 60 percent of poor families with children are headed by single mothers. In the 1960s, as the war on poverty was getting underway, the black illegitimate birth rate was 25 percent. Today, two out of three black children are born out of wedlock. In the bottom third of the black population, concentrated in our inner cities, over 80 percent of the children are born without a father who accepts responsibility for their existence. Not knowing what it is to have a father, most of them will never know what it means to be a father. The current welfare system is a monumentally wrongheaded and expensive subsidizing of the abandonment of male responsibility. This reality—and not mendacious chatter about thirty million Americans being poor—is the real crisis of poverty in our society.

Because the reality of the underclass has to do mainly with culture and patterns of personal behavior, what government can do to help is limited. Policy experts fiddle with incentives and disincentives in the welfare system, and some states are conducting experiments in linking benefits to work and job training. While they are perhaps modest steps in the right direction, these things have been tried before, to little avail. The one thing it would seem that government should be able to do is effective policing of the neighborhoods of the poor. Underclass criminality is overwhelmingly directed against other members of the underclass. To assure to all citizens the safety of their homes and streets is an elementary obligation of government that has not been discharged for decades. But law and order is hardly the whole answer. The cultural and moral efforts required to reconstruct the ethic of work, lawful behavior, and family responsibility in our inner cities lie outside the competence of government. Parental authority and habits of self-reliance must be strengthened, and, for the most part, the only available institutions for taking the lead in these tasks are the churches in these communities.

Black and Hispanic churches may seem like a very weak reed on which to lean; and they are that. But they are usually the only indigenous institutions on the scene. Regrettably, many inner-city clergy are still content to serve as a claque for a superannuated civil rights establishment that knows how to do little more than make demands for additional government funds, accompanied by a now-tiresome apocalyptic shuffle about the fire next time. These are the clergy who tend to gain the attention of the media. In the last few years, however, there are a growing number of inner-city clergy around the country who are preaching a different message. They call upon their people to abandon the delusion of revolutionizing a putatively racist society, and to take moral charge of their own lives and communities.

These clergy and their local churches deserve the supportive attention of national religious organizations, the media, and policy experts. At present, they are not getting that attention. There are no doubt several reasons for that. One reason is that social activists in the churches, as well as news executives, still operate by a mindset formed in the 1960s. According to that mindset, poor folk are supposed to rail against the injustice of society and the rest of us are to respond by feeling guilty and then appease the poor by tossing a few more welfare benefits their way. A certain style of white liberalism is expert at choreographing what are essentially black minstrel shows of fake intimidation, and some "radical" clergy are always ready to play their part. The preachers of self-reliance and moral reconstruction are declared to be "conservative," the ultimate epithet of liberal dismissiveness. In truth, they are the real reformers who are challenging the status quo that is supported by a civil rights establishment and welfare bureaucracy that, some good intentions notwithstanding, encourage the perpetual infantilizing of the inner-city poor.

If the answer to the real crisis of poverty in America is moral reconstruction led by inner-city churches and ancillary institutions, does this mean that the rest of us are let off the hook? The answer is emphatically negative. Policy changes are required to empower poor people to break out of dependency and take charge of their lives. One such change is school choice—a simple demand of justice that will give poor parents and children the same opportunities and responsibilities presently taken for granted by most other Americans who choose their schools, whether by opting out of the government school system or by moving to another community.

Genuine reform requires a careful rethinking of attitudes and policies across the board. Peter F. Drucker, doyen of business management and public policy, urges that the time has long since come to recognize that "government has proved itself incompetent at solving social problems." The answer, says Drucker, is to look to the voluntary, nonprofit organizations that have a demonstrated ability to meet human needs. The Salvation Army, Alcoholics Anonymous, Catholic Charities, and the Samaritans, are among the more than 900,000 nonprofits in the country, most of them close to their communities. Despite fashionable derision of what George Bush called the "thousand points of light," points of light are breaking out all over. Thousands of nonprofits, focused on helping those who need help, came into existence in 1990 alone.

Giving the lie to all the talk about compassion fatigue, voluntarism is breaking out all over. There are now some 90 million Americans—one out of every two adults— working as volunteers in nonprofits for an average of three hours a week. Drucker notes that nonprofits have become America's largest "employer." Brian O'Connell, head of the Independent Sector, believes that within ten years two-thirds of American adults, 120 million people, will work as nonprofit volunteers for five hours or more a week. That would mean a doubling of the hours that people devote to helping others, typically on a one-to-one basis of real support and caring. This leads Peter Drucker to a conclusion that is as compelling as it is vast in its implications: "The nonprofits have the potential to become America's social sector—equal in importance to the public sector of government and the private sector of business." To which we would add that, although generally unrecognized, the voluntary associations are already the *effective* social sector in helping disadvantaged Americans.

Drucker's analysis finds its philosophical and theological counterpart in the teachings of Pope John Paul II. In his recent encyclical *Centesimus Annus,* the key concept advanced for meeting human needs is "the subjectivity of society." That is to say, the poor and disadvantaged are always to be viewed as subjects, never as objects. The Pope lifts up the importance of "intermediate institutions"—what some social thinkers in this country call the "mediating structures"—of family, church, and voluntary associations as the chief instruments for securing individual and social assistance. He places severe strictures on the role of the state in social welfare—a role that, he says, inevitably leads to bureaucratization, depersonalization, and dependency.

Of course, all such reformist proposals are vehemently resisted by those who have a vested interest in statist control of social programs, and are most vehemently resisted by the unions of those who work for the state. Witness the desperate opposition of the National Education Association and the American Federation of

Teachers to school choice. Curiously, even leaders of the nonprofits betray a statist hostility to the concept of the subjectivity of society. A newspaper interviews an official of Catholic Charities who acknowledges that there has been a remarkable upsurge in the number of donations and volunteers for the organization's work with the homeless, drug addicts, and others in need. The monsignor is not happy about this development. "This reflects a failure of government," he says. "In a more just society, these needs would be handled through government programs." The notion that voluntary response to human need is a stopgap measure until the government can be persuaded to take over is deeply and tragically entrenched in sectors of our political culture.

Policy changes are possible that can help people to help people take charge of their lives. In education, housing, and other areas, vouchers and tax credits have an enormous potential that has hardly been explored. In addition, Drucker suggests that the government could allow taxpayers to deduct $1.10 for each dollar they give to nonprofits. "This," he says, "would solve the nonprofits' money problems at once." That may be exaggerated, but such a deduction would be a huge help. As it is, the IRS and many states are trying to penalize and curtail donations to nonprofits, and to restrict the tax exemptions essential to voluntary associations. Misguided tax policies, combined with pressure from unionized government workers, threaten to choke off what is truly a remarkable resurgence of American compassion in action.

We have it on the highest authority that the poor will always be with us. Jesus was not recommending passivity or indifference to the plight of those in need. He was stating the simple fact that, in any society and at any time, there will always be a certain number of people who will not be able to make it on their own—who, at least at times, will be in desperate need of help. Most Americans know that, and most Americans care. There is not now, and there probably never has been, a society on earth in which, without coercion, so many people do so much to help their neighbors.

That caring is abused and stifled, however, by the ideologically driven message that thirty million Americans live in poverty, and that the "crisis" is unmanageable absent a vast expansion of government bureaucracy. Caring is abused and stifled by the message that the poor are childlike dependents—objects—who cannot be expected to take charge of their lives. It is abused and stifled by the perverse notion that it counts as "compassion" when a politician votes taxpayer money for welfare programs, but it is pitifully irrelevant "charity" when someone gives five hours a week teaching an inner-city teenager to read so that he or she can get a job.

The American people are not indifferent to the question, "What should we do about the poor?" But they could become indifferent, or worse, if politicians, journalists, policy experts, and preachers continue to discount their commonsensical answers, if we continue to lie to them. There is no compassion fatigue. There is an ominous and growing mendacity fatigue.

What I have said about the opportunities of inner city churches is by no means limited to inner city churches. Christians and others who claim the covenant with Abraham need to rethink carefully the fundamental concepts associated with poverty, riches, work, and communal responsibility. Attending to the "commonsensical answers" is of critical importance, but Christians need to know that their views and actions accord with Biblical truth. Such a careful rethinking is, as I understand it, the purpose of the present book.

Nobody should expect that a study of the Bible will yield a fully elaborated set of policies for addressing the problems of poverty and the urban underclass in contemporary America. At the same time, Christian truth has everything to do with our understanding of human nature—of the incentives, aspirations, and capacities that both motor and limit human behavior. As a political matter, an approach to welfare that does not resonate with a Biblical understanding of moral duty and possibility is not going to find secure support in this confusedly "Christian" nation. Even more important, such an approach would not deserve our support. A believable and effective approach to welfare must be premised upon all that we can learn from history and our own experience as illumined by God's Word. It is my hope that the present book will contribute mightily to that end.

INTRODUCTION

David W. Hall

These essays grew out of a conference hosted by and grown from the vision of the Elders of the Covenant Presbyterian Church in Oak Ridge, Tennessee, October 23–25, 1992. They represent the mature thought of several of the most informed minds among evangelical policy analysts on the question of welfare. Although representing a diversity of opinions and perspectives, the unifying heartbeat of these essays are matters of principle and historical analysis.

In offering this set of essays, we realize that this is but a dent in a large problem, and others have offered many other fine analyses. Yet, we hope the church and thinking Christians will be strengthened and informed by these essays. It is indeed a ripe time for a thoroughgoing reform of a system which is so manifestly deficient.

We also realize that we are not the first (nor the last) to make these points. As we sought to have a sensitivity to history, in order to find the larger picture, it is appropriate to state the broad themes of this work in the words of one who addressed them a century ago. Abraham Kuyper, a shining example of properly uniting theology with political reality, himself the Prime Minister of the

Netherlands in 1900, spoke to many of the issues we had in mind. He is assuredly one of our mentors.

Only a few years ago it was exceedingly impolitic, even ideologically heretical, to criticize the sacred cow of the "Great Society," fantasized by over-active imaginations during the 1960s. To merely utter the possibility of "welfare reform" was to blaspheme against the state, as well as against a wrongly conceived notion of compassion. These prophetic authors are now conscience-bound to cry down a prominent error of our times. Yet, even secular critics are making our job easier, as a welfare reform movement is budding, the likes of which lends hope to these contributors. Whereas several years ago hardly anyone was speaking of welfare reform, the economic and moral fruit of the past 30 years' practice of ministering to the poor definitively rebuts the notion that the compassionate thing to do for the poor is to continue welfare as we know it. Hence, we propose a truly compassionate approach, shared with both believer and unbeliever, in the sure confidence that our Creator knows best how His Creatures will thrive. To love our neighbor as ourself is to call for and advocate welfare reform. We can do no less.

As we offer our work to the church and to the world, I want to express my deep thanks to George Grant, David Dunham, and the excellent staff at Legacy Communications for editorial improvements. It is a pleasure to work with such gifted craftsmen, who serve the Lord with such vigor, style, and grace. I'm thankful for the work and encouragement by the staff and editors at Presbyterian and Reformed, as well. I have also been indebted to the work of other conference participants whose writing is not in this present volume. I'm thankful to Randy Nabors, whose life, example, and thought have both pricked my conscience and also challenged me; to Joel Belz for his faithfulness and hearty commitment to see this issue and all others captive to the Lordship of Christ; to Hilton Terrell, for his fine and consistent grappling with related issues of health care and medical ethics; to Michael Cromartie for his wise suggestions and seasoned leadership in our work sessions; and to Mark Buckner for technical assistance, as well as advice on this and many other projects. However, of all people involved, I want to thank my fellow elder Robert Dotson for shepherding the Conference, as well as for his unabating concern for this entire area of mercy ministries.

Part I

THE PRESENT STATE OF THE WELFARE STATE: THE NEED FOR REFORM

1. TOWARD A POST-STATIST THEOLOGICAL ANALYSIS OF POVERTY

David W. Hall

The opening essay by David Hall, Pastor of Covenant Presbyterian Church in Oak Ridge, TN, asks if it is not a proper time to re-evaluate welfare, this time from a non-statist perspective. Summaries of studies from the past decade are reported, along with an exhortation to construct policy without ignoring eternal norms. Three primary questions are posed: (1) If our present system is so flawed, is there any inherent reason to automatically reject a theologically based model?; (2) Does the Bible address this subject?; and (3) What guidance does the Bible give us for this modern debate?

It is conceivable that the modern threat to human society, to put it bluntly, arises less from chaos than from an overabundance of state order, a political superorganization which acts as an institutional buffer to isolate men from one another, de-personalize them, . . . and turn love of neighbor into a welfare machine. The problem can perhaps be clarified in terms of the parable of the Good Samaritan. . . . Does not the Samaritan's ministry of mercy become inconceivable, is it not altered in its very substance, the moment it is institutionalized, put into the hands of a 'Good Samaritans' League', e.g., or even into the hands of the state itself? Is it not thereby robbed of its very point? . . . Can the Good Samaritan be envisaged as a welfare officer?[1]

When even unbelievers recognize the failure of a broken system, it is a shame for the church to be the last to see the problem, if it is one addressed by the canon of Scripture. In our own culture, we now have several states insinuating that the welfare state created in the 1960s is broken. The statist approach to welfare—although a sacred cow, often above even the slightest criticism—may in the end be just as ill-founded and impossible as the statist approach to economics (in the former Soviet Union). For some time now, some Christians have protested that the present welfare approach is flawed at the fundamental level of principle. Thus far, however, policy experts in our country have refused to learn from or be influenced by religious considerations, which could be laid at the foundation of a more successful approach to the care for the poor. It may just now be that the myth of the absolute noninfluence of the church on the state is showing its deficiency in this, one of its chief laboratories of social experimentation. Welfare without the contour of spiritual and ethical values is the poorer for it.

Only recently have the states of California, Georgia, Wisconsin, Michigan, New Jersey, and Massachusetts proposed and sought to implement welfare reform. The culmination of this new wave seemed to crest at the July 1992 Democratic National Convention, at which the Democratic Party adopted a platform that called for welfare reform, including a proviso that no more than two years of welfare payments be given without recipients finding or returning to work.[2] In most cases, Biblical Christians find themselves welcoming these reforms as improvements. Is that an accident, or is there Biblical justification for possible rapprochement between a Biblical approach to welfare and the state-proposed reforms? This author thinks that it is no coincidence, but that indeed what may be happening is that certain commonsensical secular groups are being driven by the created realities to come into a closer conformity to the principles for caring for the materially poor revealed all along in Scripture. If that is the case, those who have provided Biblical critiques of the Great Society approach may be in the position of not only being vindicated, but more importantly, being able to shed light on some of the solutions—if it can first truly be admitted that the pre-existing system is beyond repair. One good first step is for the church and state to work together, each with integrity in and according to its own sphere, but no longer as divorced partners. It is high time that the church recaptured her rightful role in society, and high time that the government ceased locking her out, especially in areas where the church has divine mandate, divine methods, and practical efficacy. We contend that the most helpful ally the state can have is a strong, Biblically-based church, living out the fullness of the Gospel in word and deed.

If Federal and state governments are seeing the defects of a corrupt system and welcoming the renewed contributions by other agents of responsible charity, this may be an opportune moment for the Christian to contribute models and policy. This *knowledge base* is seldom considered in policy matters, yet speaks from a non-partisan platform which promises superior information. So if a system which excluded divine principles is now recognized as broken, that should not surprise us. We should have expected its eventual collapse (as with the 74-year-old experiment in the Soviet Union) and be prepared to model a more durable and effective method of welfare. Those Christians who have been rather uncritical of the statist welfare approach may even feel some of the red-facedness felt by those theologians who yoked themselves to a Marxist-liberationist approach. Once the foundational principles crumble, the whole house of cards soon collapses. Following the evident failure of statism to provide in either the realm of economics or welfare, one can hardly expect success from various recycled statist variations on the original theme.

Appeals Court Justice Alex Kozinski recently commented on the "dark lessons of Utopia," which are inexplicably ignored by many policy analysts. Commenting on how "they just don't get it," Kozinski notes:

> Events in Eastern Europe over the last few years should prove an embarrassment to many. People in this country

should be reconsidering their fundamental assumptions about what government can and should do, and what it should not. Surprisingly, this has not happened. Government at all levels grows bigger and more powerful; it absorbs more of our productive resources than ever before; and its involvement in our daily lives increases unabated. Even as the peoples of Eastern Europe strive to establish free market economies, implement private property rights, and diminish the role of government, the United States continues on a path headed in the opposite direction.[3]

Professor Michael Kelley warns of this creeping socialism, as it effects governmental programs (of which welfare is but one instance): "Even though government today dominates every facet of life and society, and reaches deeply, even perversely, into the pockets of its citizens, there has been a persistent refusal by politicians, pundits, interest groups and the media to call this enormous growth in government 'socialism.' "[4] Perhaps it is high time to confess that the vast majority of American welfare in the past generation has been founded more on the ideological premises of socialism—complete with its views of man, society, and eschatology—than Christians can Biblically affirm. Why merely seek to keep a dead patient alive on life support? It is time for Christians to bury the cadavers of statism and socialism, even if propped up in the garments of U.S. welfare. If it walks like a socialist program and quacks like a socialist program, it is most likely a socialist duck, even if called by any other name.

Recently, historian Paul Johnson commented on the massive wave of privatization (with the privatization of state-owned enterprises valued at nearly $50 billion in 1991, nearly double the amount of 1990) with clarity:

> The question future historians will ask is not why politicians and public opinion turned against the welfare state, but why it took them so long. Indeed, if ever a theory has been tested and disproved, it is that of the all-powerful, all-benevolent state—a theory that has led in practice to wars great and small, to the death of millions of people and to the scorching of entire economies and environments. Never before has mankind created such an all-consuming monster. In both its totalitarian and social-democratic versions, it has proved efficient in nothing except a capacity to squander resources and lives.[5]

We may even be ready to admit that "Unheavenly Cities" are the primary by-products of this social experimentation, and agree that even secular social analysis "demonstrates with utmost cogency that the vast majority of Great Society programs begun in the 1960s and slavishly funded ever since have relegated many of the urban poor to hopeless, disorganized lives of extraordinary squalor and violence."[6] Perhaps the church will wait no longer to prophetically speak to these issues, from an unadulterated perspective of divine revelation, lest we fall even further behind the insights of those around us who do not necessarily avail themselves to divine authority. It may be more timely than ever, in light of the recently failed experiment with socialism, to hear the caveat from not-so-conservative priest, Andrew Greeley, who warned in 1985 that on these subjects the church must be most careful not to render itself dated by simply echoing "the fashionable liberalism of five years ago, whenever five years ago was. They will arrive on the scene, as always, a little breathless and a little late."[7]

It might be helpful to distinguish from the outset what kind of welfare approach is deemed irreparable. Marvin Olasky[8] suggests three distinct eras of welfare in the U.S.

The *first* type, pre-FDR, was classical, in which most of the responsibility for welfare devolved on the private and charitable sectors. In this era, the church and other mediating structures played a leading role in welfare, emphasizing "personal involvement of giver and recipient, and tried to work on spiritual as well as material needs." The *second* type was modern (ca 1930–1960), with the government leading the way to help the needy poor, as exceptions to the rule, and that temporarily so. The *third* type began in the early 1960s and created a nearly permanent underclass of continually dependent people. Olasky speaks of this as the post-modern approach, characterized by "welfare rights" under the "omni-entitlement banner."

In our time we see the crumbling of this third type, the Great Society experiment of the 60s. After a generation of experimentation, we (and some brave policy leaders) can now say the experiment has failed. When the statistics considered later document how never before has so much been spent to accomplish so little as in the last 30 years, and how this has not improved but diminished the plight of the deserving poor, it is difficult to aspire to argue the contentions of Great Society welfare. It will be more constructive to bury the corpse of statism, stop the denial of its death, even eulogize it, if you will, but move on in pursuit of better alternatives learning from failed systems.

Since the mid-70s our government has spent in excess of two hundred billion dollars per year for poverty relief. As Charles Murray notes, "After all the trillions of dollars spent on welfare from 1965 to date, 14.4 percent of our population (33.7 million persons) still live below the poverty line. . . . In 1950, 1-in-12 Americans were below the poverty line; in 1979, it was 1-in-9; today, 1-in-every-7 Americans is reported to be below the poverty line."[9] Further we see that the heart of this 1960–1990 experiment was the assumption of the notion that, "Poverty was not created by one's own lack of skill, training, or initiative, or even by temporary bad luck. The problem was *the system*. It was racist, anti-black, and anti-poor. Therefore it would do no good to lend the poor a helping hand, since the system was against them."[10]

George Grant summarizes that "almost thirty-five million Americans are perennially poverty-stricken. More than 10 percent of the White population, 30 percent of the Black population, and 25 percent of all Hispanics have become part of our society's permanent underclass. More than one-fourth of all American children and almost 80 percent of elderly women living alone live in poverty, all too often in abject poverty. Despite the fact that one out of every five citizens receives some kind of means-tested public welfare, the stranglehold that poverty wields in their lives intensifies with every passing day."[11] Furthermore, Grant calls to our attention "the feminization of poverty" in that, "More than seventy percent of women in the labor force today work out of economic necessity . . . An astonishing 75 percent of this nation's poverty is borne by women and their children . . . the number of women who headed poor families has increased nearly 40 percent."[12]

Charles Murray notes, "Overall civilian social costs increased by 20 times from 1950 to 1980, in constant dollars. During that same period the United States population increased by half."[13] Moreover, it is noted that, "Since 1950, the number of persons receiving public and social welfare payments has increased from six million to 18 million [in 1974] to more than 30 million [in 1984]. Aid to families with dependent children (AFDC payments) soared from 3.5 billion dollars in 1960 to 16.1

billion dollars in 1984; the amount spent on food stamps increased from 550 million to 10.7 billion dollars. In 1983 . . . , all governments spent 455.8 billion dollars for public assistance and social welfare; that represented 39 percent of all government spending and 15 percent of the GNP. In 1984, welfare expenditures accounted for some 64 percent of the Federal Budget."[14] Add to this that: "Federal social spending rose by nearly 10 per cent in real terms during the Reagan years, and another 20 per cent during the first three Bush years. Throughout the 1980s these programs accounted for more than half of all spending."[15]

When one asks has all of this expenditure-oriented approach helped, it can be noted that in 1965 there were less than a quarter million illegitimate births to blacks and yet after some 20 years of social engineering (a generation to those bearing illegitimate children) it was reported that, "In 1980 48 percent of live births among blacks were to single women compared with 17 percent in 1950.[16] Further escalating, by 1988 63.5 per cent of all black babies were born out of wedlock."[17]

Emphasizing that "Poverty is not primarily a problem for the state," and that "Poverty is more a *human* than a monetary problem. Helping the poor to acquire the skills of productive economic independence demands far more from us than mere monetary gains."[18] An earlier response by the Catholic Lay Commission observed in 1985 that, "If the poverty shortfall of $45 billion were simply *given* to the poor, that would of course temporarily lift all above the poverty line as defined by the Census Bureau."[19] The sheer amounts of money expended on welfare don't seem to be eradicating poverty; rather these gargantuan amounts seem unable really to assist the truly needy. As Michael Novak puts it in perspective, the ratio of spending on welfare programs increased *twenty-one* times from 1950 to 1980,[20] while population increased only about two-fold, thus concluding that the very *design* of welfare public policy is faulty. As further proof of the irreparable estate of U.S. welfare policy, Novak compares the aggregate sum of money needed to lift all those below the poverty line to a level above the poverty line ($45 billion) to the actual expenses on such welfare programs for 1982 ($390 billion). His obvious inference is that our welfare approach has broad abuse, and is not currently reaching the truly needy. This observation was made ten years ago, eight years before socialism was more clearly seen for its bankruptcy. The question is why, in light of the abject failure of statist systems, is this still not reformed?

Steven Moore has noted that, "Welfare roles have skyrocketed from two million families in 1970 to 3.5 million in 1980 to 4.6 million in 1990. The child of a parent on welfare is three times more likely to be on welfare as an adult."[21] And he notes that Governor Tommy Thompson says, "The tragedy of the welfare state is not how much it costs, but how little progress it has bought."[22] In addition Moore notes that to the degree that state governments down-sized, the actual benefit to recipients of welfare grew. Moore notes that the segment which is most benefitted by this explosion in welfare expenditures is not the private sector, but indeed government employees. He says, "Between 1980 and 1990 the rate of increase of pay and benefits grew an incredible four times faster than the private sector of compensation. Meanwhile, work forces collecting these salaries mushroomed: While the U.S. population grew 9 percent, state public employment grew 20 percent."[23]

In *Bringing in the Sheaves,* George Grant compares the expenditures on welfare as follows: "It [HEW] began with a budget of two billion dollars, actually a modest amount, less than 5 percent of the expenditures on national defense. Fifteen years later, however, its budget had soared to 180 billion dollars, one-and-a-half times more than the total spent by the Army, the Navy, and the Air Force. In fact, its budget had grown to be the third largest in the world, exceeded only by the entire budget of the United States government and that of the Soviet Union."[24] Sadly, with the disintegration of the former Soviet Union, the U.S. can boast of funding *both* of the two largest budgets in the world: (1) the entire budget of the U.S. government, and (2) the combined budgets of HEW.

And such expansion was not limited to administrations of only one party. The Food Stamp expenditures quadrupled between 1965 and 1967, while "Under Nixon, that number was again quadrupled. And, by 1980, the number of beneficiaries had grown to nearly twenty-two million, fifty times the coverage of Johnson's original war on poverty legislative package."[25] Further, even during the Reagan years of 1984–1988, the welfare budgets increased "more than one hundred fifty billion dollars. So, despite all the liberal moaning and groaning and the media hype . . . it is obvious that the only thing Reagan cut was the rate of increasing in spending. . . . In less than twenty years, the war on poverty had ceased to be an innovation and had become an institution. It had, indeed, become 'unconditional'."[26] This phenomena continued on into the early 1990s, despite Republican protestations to the contrary. So much did these continue, that eventually the State Treasuries began to approach bankruptcy (as in California in the late summer of 1992), and it was becoming apparent that welfare, as it presently existed, was insolvent. As Grant recaps, "on the way to Utopia" from the 1960s to the 1980s "social welfare spending increased more than twenty times,"[27] and it was hard for anyone to maintain that actual progress was being made or that statism was working.

Moreover, as economist Walter Williams has remarked, "The money spent on poverty programs since the 1960s could have bought the entire assets of the Fortune 500 companies and virtually all the U.S. farmland."[28] It is still more shocking to note that,

> Despite a great society effort now well into its third decade—the cost of more than 2.5 trillion dollars—the life of many inner city residents has never been worse, for blacks especially. Today blacks comprise almost half of the prison population. The homicide rate for black males age 15–24 has increased by 40 percent since the mid-1980s, and is now the leading cause of death for that age group. Forty percent of those murdered in the U.S. are black men killed by other black men. Sixty-five percent of all black babies are born to unwed mothers; the number is as high as 80 percent in many inner cities.[29]

As William Bennett notes the failure of these systems, he says that the supposed leftist "Champions of the poor keep recycling the same stale, failed proposals of the past. They are increasingly irrelevant to the debate."[30] With these foregoing critiques, shall the church recycle the same "failed proposals of the past," mirroring that irrelevance? Or does it have some unique contribution to make in the post-statist era?

Oddly, at present, the welfare liberals are much like traditional reactionaries of the 1950s, clinging to established ways that are looking more antiquated as time passes. I can still hear the echoes of 1960s-ish first generation welfarists cheering for the rest of society to catch up with the latest results of their new studies and tests. In our times it is embarrassing to fall behind the learning curve, contending for old, disproven theories. Very few astronomers endorse a scientific platform to restructure NASA, based on a flat-earth model. Yet strangely, a similarly reactionary appearance is the visage worn by those who keep pleading for welfare to "Do more of the same," or "Stay the course." The oddity of this role reversal, with some conservatives leading the way and actually proposing new forms, is certain to add to the perplexity of those who still dogmatically cling to a broken-down statist-welfarist model. Although there is definitely room for improvement, one seldom hears the fact which Michael Novak cites, to wit, "Even the 28 million blacks in the U.S., arguably the worst-off of the U.S. population, have a cumulative income (\$200 billion) larger than the gross domestic product of all but nine other nations of the world."[31]

About a generation after the Soviet experiment had been tried (and found wanting), there were some who prophetically announced its dead end and eventual demise, only to end up in gulags. Let us hope that in our own society, various theoreticians will not be so dogmatic as to martyr those who speak out for a better system. Indeed, the U.S. Great Society statism is nearly as bankrupt as the Soviet experiment. We may have the historic opportunity to learn from their errors. It would perhaps be an even greater error not only to fail to learn from another empire's statist defeat, but furthermore to exile those who are critical of it. Even if not politically correct, it is hoped that some will have "ears to hear" and that some will nondogmatically listen to helpful solutions for welfare reform.

One quarter is routinely excluded from this normal dialogue, and that sector is the orthodox Christian church. Few societies would so easily reject the historic faith of their citizens, as ours has. Yet, since 1960, not only has God been ejected from the classroom, but also from the policy-making conferences and offices of social welfare providers. Isn't it high time to admit (as some governors are, largely due to economic laws) that indeed the system has failed? If we can admit that, then the obvious challenges to any group is to *find other episte-mological data bases for reform,* and to be informed by different sources. *If the tried sources have failed, perhaps the moment is ripe to consider other sources, options, and norms.* Quite possibly a model which does not isolate the church from the state might be more constructive than the post-modern approach to welfare.

Let me then, on the assumption that with the collapse of statist models will come an open-minded consideration of post- or non-statist models, pose three questions:

First Question

Could the Bible's revealed set of religious norms on the subject of welfare and its proper structure be a primary source for the reformation of welfare in our own times? After all, if other sources have failed miserably, is there inherent reason to disqualify from consideration a set of normative and didactic instructions which purports to have superior knowledge? Specifically, is there justification for *not* considering the information from Biblical teaching—at least on par (if not more worthy) than the approaches of the anthropology, sociology, and economics of modernity, especially in light of their proven failure rate?

A theological analysis of poverty is needed in the first place. Among the many analyses of poverty, especially in the 20th century, there have been two primary categories of social approach to poverty—the first being the socialist, and the second being the capitalist. The socialist experiment has now collapsed, and although it was an attempt to create a sense of equity for those who were impoverished or downtrodden, nonetheless the communal experiment has proven itself to be faulty in economics. Neither did it help alleviate poverty. To continue in the socialist vein, in light of the practitioners' own confessions, is like persistently trying to build a reactionary physic upon a platform of a publicly witnessed and failed metaphysic.

The second approach was a post-1960 Great Society approach (Lyndon Johnson and others). In this approach to poverty many tried to use the welfare state and, through redistribution of assets, spread the wealth. As a result there have been a number of types of analysis of phenomenon of poverty. For example, there have been anthropological, sociological (Michael Harrington's *The Other America*), economical, evangelical (Ron Sider and the *Sojourners* magazine for example), and soon there will even be (if there is not already) ecological analyses of poverty.

All of these have one perspectival dynamic in common: they *a priori* begin "from below," and addressing the realities of poverty, seek to explain or analyze them in terms of the person, the society, the economic, ecological, or even religious structure. All of these are antirevelational, unidimensional, and limited to the sum total of wisdom possessed by fallible and self-interested observers. These may be classified as *anthropological*. However, in light of all of this—even with treatments of poverty by evangelicals in the last twenty years (See Ron Sider, for example)—still, there are very few *theological* analyses of poverty—those which treat poverty "from above" or from a Scriptural perspective.

And of those very few theological analyses (see, for example, the 1985 Pastoral Letter of the Roman Catholic Bishops and several statements of the General Assembly of the PCUSA), most of those have been decidedly liberal and normally antithetic to Western economics. To our disgrace, of all the attempts to theologize about poverty in U.S.A. churches, the vast majority have been sponsored by decidedly liberal groups whose methodology is more compatible with the above secular or anthropological analyses than with Scripture. Hence, even most of the purportedly "from above" studies have been only *slightly from above* or a baptized "from below" approach, certainly not from a radically transcendent perspective.

Ronald Nash also comments to the point of the normal expertise of these 'pastoral commentators' as he cites a previous study in which the author "discovered that the typical Catholic Bishop whose authority is being used to support debatable economic policies knows less about economics than a college freshman in the third week of a basic economic course."[32] It is less likely that Protestant bishops have any greater expertise. Nash summarizes that, "While the Catholic bishops use the Bible to show that God is a *very* liberal Democrat,[33] the liberation theologians use the Bible to show that God is a Marxist."[34] Nash bemoans the reality that most of our religious economists-come-lately exhibit a "misunderstanding of capitalism only exceeded by [their] fanaticism. . . . For Christians like this, capitalism is supposed to be un-Christian or anti-Christian because it allegedly gives a predominant place to greed or other un-Christian values."[35] And P. T. Bauer incisively sums up that all too often in purported Christian studies of these complex issues,

> Even the eternal verities are overlooked. The responsibility of a person for the consequences of his actions and the fundamental distinction between mankind and the rest of creation are basic Christian tenets. They are pertinent [to these issues] . . . but they are ignored throughout these documents. . . . People who pronounce on matters about which they are ignorant are apt simply to absorb ideas propagated or taken up by other elite or establishment groups. Nature abhors a vacuum not only in the physical world but also in the world of politics and ideas.[36]

Hence, not only will we be in search of Biblical treatises on this subject, but moreover, we are now in a position to strenuously avoid certain liberal approaches to this area which do not stand up to mature hermeneutical scrutiny. Many have been tried and found wanting. We may in the end find that due to philosophical presuppositions and ideological policy precommitments, many of the purported Christian studies about the poor and welfare reflect much more of the prevailing Great Society assumptions than the Scriptures really contain. It is an opportune moment to ask, "Do the Scriptures really urge or sanction the implementation of the LBJ Great Society? Or are those assumptions more akin to the wishful thinking of mid-20th century liberal utopianism in the U.S.A.? Is this a case of Christ or culture determining?"

Even Andrew Greeley has described this as "little more than a rehash of the party-line liberal conventional wisdom of five to fifteen years ago, . . . pop-Marxism . . . religious underpinning for the latter-day New Deal of the

1980 Democratic party platform . . . differ[ing] only marginally from suggestions one could have gleaned from the op-ed pages of liberal publications in the late 1970s and very early 1980s."[37] Peter Berger even estimates that the Catholic Bishops' Letter corresponded "remarkably with the agenda proposed by the Democratic party platform of 1984."[38] Nash again summarizes the situation well (he refers to it as "a growing extremism"): "The Bible has become an important weapon in the hands of those who seek a Christian justification for economic and political positions that dismiss capitalism as anti-Christian. Many writings from the Christian Left illustrate a proof-text approach to the Bible. What these writers normally do is isolate some vague passage (usually from the Old Testament) that pertains to an extinct cultural situation or practice. They then proceed to 'deduce' some complex economic or political program from that text. In the process, they exhibit an attachment to a mind-boggling method of Biblical interpretation."[39]

It should soon be admitted (or discovered) that any and all welfare systems are based on pre-conceived values. In fact, no social program is isolated from its underlying world view. A philosophical world view is the interpretive matrix for all these studies—ours included.

William J. Bennett has gone so far as to say (in reference to John Paul II's encyclical *Centesimus Annus*), "The theological dimension is needed both for interpreting and solving present-day problems in human society. . . . If there is not ultimate truth to guide and direct political activity, then ideas and convictions can easily be manipulated for reasons of power. As history demonstrates, a democracy without values turns into open or thinly disguised totalitarianism."[40]

William Willimon has recently reiterated the importance of a worldview in considering welfare options, as he says:

> All philanthropy proceeds from a world view. The Nazis had an extensive system of social welfare. When Nazi doctors helped to exterminate those who were judged to be 'mentally defective', they did so out of philanthropic motive. They saw themselves not as doing evil but as doing good to those who were 'less fortunate'. Likewise, the President who supported changes in the national welfare program because, 'Such changes will remove the poor from welfare rolls and make them taxpayers', could also be said to be acting from philanthropic motives. *Christian* philanthropy arises from our claims about the nature of God. The parables that Jesus told were meant to depict a God who is by our standards, effusive, extravagant, and therefore odd. *Christian* philanthropy ought to proceed from this odd depiction of the way the world is.[41]

The point is that all welfare is inescapably rooted in a world view, and in practical consequence. If either fails, so will the system. It is a difficult, but imperative task that we relegate failed approaches to the same trash heap as other broken systems, if indeed, earlier liberal and statist attempts at this were in reality philosophy masked as Scriptural study. We see too clearly that conservatives are not the only ones who occasionally plaster Biblical proof-texts over their already presupposed political ideology. Indeed, in our generation, liberal American mainline Christians have exhibited an eery proximity to the cultural mores of statist liberalism. It is hard to attribute to coincidence alone the almost lock-step agreement of the National Council of Churches with the welfarism of the Left. Of course, we must guard against the same tendency in our own study.

All in all, however, it seems that a definite affirmative answer to this first question does justify a study originating from an orthodox Scriptural point of view. It is at least worth exploring whether or not a religious set of principles might help to reform welfare. It's hard to think they could be either more dangerous or less successful than the foregoing plans. A "from above" study could hardly go further afield than the present system.

Second Question

If then, we are open to the possibility that the Bible has something normative "from above" to say to this arena, we have to then query, "Does the Bible actually address this subject?" It may be well and good to acknowledge the potential for Biblical information, or for religious mores to have a shaping influence on societal policy. Yet all the while, if that corpus of sacred Scripture does not address the subject, we are left with a null set—as far as helpfulness.

So, let us ask, "Does the Bible treat this subject?" The answer from nearly all quarters of the theological spectrum would be *yes*. Both conservatives and liberals may actually agree on this question. Few would dispute that the Bible does at least minimally concern itself with the plight of the poor, with the need for compassion, and with the vague principles of guidance on this whole complex of questions. It even appears that the Bible does address the issues of welfare structures, and itself provides some. There are, in short, Biblical vehicles of welfare. For example, from the earliest of times, in the Old Testament, God charges the family with the responsibility, of caring for its own and its disadvantaged. Indeed, the family comes first in the development of solutions, by hundreds of years. Actually the "state" is not even a creation ordinance, nor even formally regulated until about 1400 B.C. at Sinai. Hence, we will be sensitive to those established priorities, and seek to structure any welfare reform accordingly. Throughout, it will be maintained that the family is responsible as the first arena of alleviation for the needs of its own members.

The Old Testament is particularly ripe with welfare vehicles, as it established the Levirate, gleaning, and other family-based vehicles. It must suffice, for now, to note that there are priorities of sphere responsibility, and contrary to the "Great Society" model, the state does not serve as the first bastion of welfare provision, the family does. In fact, early on, there is no state welfare—only family. For whole millennia, civilization was able to thrive without statist welfare. Hence, such principle must be factored into any proposed reform. The Bible is actually full of information and norms for this. So, yes, it does address the subject in a creative way, which is non-duplicative of any other modern approach. The only question is to what degree, and with which proper hermeneutical particularities does the Bible speak.

Third Question

Hence, the remaining, and pressing question is, "On the supposition that the Bible does and should speak to this societal issue, just what are the specifics of the Biblical teaching on the proper administration of welfare?" That is the question to which most of these essays are addressed.

In the following essays and analyses, honest attempts are made to cull some of the most overt Biblical teachings on this subject, and set forth theological and normative propositions that may be drawn upon to inform any attempt at welfare reform. In so doing, it is admitted from the outset that these are neither final nor free from bias. Others have also made honest attempts at this in the past, with varying degrees of Biblical accuracy.[42] It is intended that the teachings of Scripture have more influence in the formation of these principles than the political or social views of this or any author. If that is not the case, this study will be in vain. It is no contribution to an already bloated field of studies to merely replicate the previous ideologies in the various disciplines. If the Scriptural sourcing for this issue is of any value, it is of value precisely to the degree that the revealed principles themselves are elaborated, instead of elaborating the pre-existing policy commitments of any author.

2. REAL WELFARE REFORM: AN IDEA WHOSE TIME HAS COME

Doug Bandow

Author and syndicated columnist Doug Bandow provides his customarily well-researched and Biblically faithful insights to welfare reform in this short study documenting the failure of modern welfare practices in the U.S.A. Updating readers on the latest innovations—as well as the continuing failures of a tattered and worn-out approach to caring for the poor—his alternative is a private charity approach in place of the old and failed wineskins of welfare. In this short, but most salient essay, Bandow reminds us where we may expect true compassion to bear fruit—not from state-sponsored systems, but from individually and religious-based charity.

> *Luckily, government is not the only source of authority. In every community there are agencies of moral and cultural development that seek to shape the ways in which individuals conceive of their duties to themselves, their obligations to each other, and their responsibilities before God. . . . The family and the church are primary among these. These institutions have too often broken down in the inner city; they have been overwhelmed by an array of forces from within and without. Yet these are the natural sources of legitimate moral teaching—indeed, the only sources. If those institutions are not restored, the behavioral problems of the ghetto will not be overcome.*[1]

*F*or all of the partisanship and rancor in politics today, there is very little debate about the central reality of modern society: the welfare state. Originally developed in Germany and Great Britain in the last century, state social programs have arisen and expanded in every industrialized nation. Broadly defined (beyond a dole for the poor), "welfare" now accounts for not only the largest share of government spending around the industrialized world, but also the fastest growing segment of outlays, greatly contributing to the rapidly accelerating fiscal deficits that beset so many nations.

Welfare programs continue to expand because they tend to be politically sacrosanct, defended by conservatives and liberals alike. Nevertheless, in recent years dissatisfaction has been growing with programs specifically directed at the poor, with a consensus seeming to develop that such programs as Aid to Families with Dependent Children (AFDC) have "failed." In general, critics argue that these forms of welfare have not achieved their goals of poverty reduction and personal independence. To the contrary, an increasing number of observers charge, these programs have had the unintended effect of actually worsening poverty—both encouraging more people to end up poor and creating a class of people permanently dependent on the government.

In contrast, the traditional criticism of poverty programs by mainstream analysts and politicians is that they are underfunded or suffer from one or another technical problem. More recently, attention has focused on the perverse incentives created by government aid. Ongoing legislative reform efforts are now focusing on changing the behavior of welfare recipients—mandating job training and work, encouraging school attendance, discouraging additional pregnancies, etc.

Some analysts on both the right and left have gone further, however, arguing that the very design of the current system is flawed; indeed, some contend that no form of public subsidy can avoid the debilitating problems now so evident in the American inner city. Examples of the latter more "radical" skeptics of welfare include Frances Fox Piven and Richard Cloward, who contend that the *unstated* objectives of the system are illegitimate, with the government intending to control and manipulate the poor rather than help them. Starting from a very different position is Charles Murray, who argues that control and manipulation is the ultimate outcome despite the generally good intentions of legislators and administrators.

Although a sharp debate over welfare policy developed in the mid-1980s, such criticism of government poverty relief efforts is familiar to social historians. This discussion has occurred before—in Britain in the 1830s, 1880s, and 1890s, and America in the 1880s and 1890s. Alas, each new debate cycle seems to take place in a historical vacuum, with participants apparently unaware of the previous discussion.

Moreover, the professional literature is full of controversies that are highly abstruse and technical. Although important, these sub debates about a single tree all too often divert attention from efforts to better understand the forest as a whole. It is therefore better to start from the other direction, first surveying the broad assumptions and objectives that underlie government welfare policy, before attempting to resolve narrower points.

Perhaps the most basic question, especially for those of us approaching the issue from a religious perspective, is why a welfare system? Do people have a duty to help those in need? Do individuals have a *right* to aid from their better-off neighbors? If they do, which individuals may enforce a claim to welfare? The proverbial widows and orphans? Teenage mothers who choose not to work? The unemployed?

Moreover, if "society" is to act, in what form should aid be provided? Today, "compassion" is commonly equated with government social spending, yet, as Marvin Olasky details in his book *The Tragedy of American Compassion,* compassion originally meant to suffer with another. In the early years of the American republic, people created an effective, community-based safety net, one that relied on personal involvement rather than bureaucratic action. Why did the nation move from private to state provision of poverty relief?

To help answer this question Murray attempts to explain the purpose of the welfare system: what do those

who are paying the bills hope to achieve? The answers
are many and complex. Some people simply hope to buy
social stability; others want to promote economic equality; still others intend to enable people to participate fully
in society and fulfill their potential as human beings.
Whether or not these are good goals, and whether or not
they warrant coercing taxpayers to pay for a welfare program, are ultimately moral questions. The purposes of
poverty programs also raise numerous practical issues,
particularly as to the best means of achieving the system's ends. Only after we decide what we hope to
achieve can we design programs to meet those goals.

For instance, if our objective is social control rather
than personal independence, then the current programs
work pretty well. If, however, our primary objective is to
relieve human suffering, then the system's effectiveness
is much less clear: while AFDC ensures that fatherless
families do not starve, it makes fatherless families more
likely and displaces alternative sources of financial support. As for making poor people independent, the current
programs are a dismal failure. Indeed, the federal "war
on poverty," despite the expenditure of *$2 trillion* since
1965, does not even appear to have reduced the incidence
of poverty. It is probably for this reason that welfare has
long been perhaps the least popular government program.
Although most Americans want to help the less fortunate, they suspect that the government is more interested
in spending money on an expansive bureaucracy than in
making poor people independent.

The official poverty rate, now about 13.5 percent, fell
during the early 1960s but has remained essentially un-
changed since the advent of President Lyndon Johnson's
"Great Society" and concomitant expansion of the welfare state. In terms of simple numbers, the welfare roles

have expanded across the nation since inauguration of the poverty war. The 1970s were years of growth, with the number of AFDC (Aid to Families with Dependent Children) recipients rising from nearly two million to more than 3.5 million. The number of welfare recipients dipped in 1982 before rising again. But by 1990 the number of AFDC recipients nationwide was 4.6 million. A variety of other welfare programs have also shown dramatic growth over the last two decades.

Welfare outlays, though not as great as many people assume, are still substantial. In 1990, the federal government spent $210 billion on a range of welfare programs, including cash aid and medical assistance. States and localities spend billions of dollars more. The problem is particularly serious in such states as California, Michigan, and New York. California, for instance, has twice as many welfare recipients as any other state. Welfare outlays absorb about ten percent of the state's budget and are growing 12 percent a year. With benefit levels almost twice the national median, California has been attracting welfare immigrants. The state has 12 percent of the nation's population, but hosts 16 percent of AFDC beneficiaries and accounts for 26 percent of AFDC's costs nationwide. Faced with a serious budget crisis two years in a row, welfare has become a prime target for cuts.

In fact, Governor Pete Wilson placed on the November 1992 ballot an initiative to cut general benefits by up to 25 percent, end the practice of paying recipients more for additional children, and requiring teenage mothers to live with their families and stay in school to collect checks. The measure also limited migrants to their old benefit levels for a year. Wilson predicted a savings of some $600 million annually, but voters defeated the initiative out of concern over its expansion of gubernatorial power.

And California is not alone in targeting welfare. In late January, 1992, New York Governor Mario Cuomo announced his intention to cut $1 billion in welfare costs. All told, 36 states have allowed inflation to reduce real AFDC benefits; seven states have cut payments while another nine have tightened eligibility standards for the program, which primarily serves single parents with minor children. Michigan has ended so-called general assistance for able-bodied single adults, dropping 82,000 from the roles. Another dozen states have sharply cut these payments.

Moreover, in January of 1992, New Jersey ended supplemental payments for larger families. The chief legislative sponsor, then-Majority Leader Wayne Bryant, explained that: "What this does is give welfare recipients a choice. They either can have additional children and work to pay the added costs, or they can decide not to have any more children." Several states are also considering joining New Jersey in tying behavior, such as accepting employment training or working in public service jobs ("workfare") and children's attendance in school ("learnfare"), to benefits.

The Bush administration generally avoided the welfare debate while pouring ever more money into federal social programs. Spending increases on AFDC, Head Start, and Medicaid were far greater than those under Jimmy Carter or Ronald Reagan. But in future years, political conservatives may try to turn welfare policy into a serious issue in an attempt to harness the resentment of middle-class taxpayers against the party most perceived to represent the special interests, the Democrats. Even a Democrat like Bill Clinton, perceived to be more moderate than many past Democrats, might find himself under fire on this issue. During the 1992 primaries, candidate Clinton denounced the New Jersey reform package advanced by a black legislator representing the state's poorest district, stating that he would instead spend more money on education and child care. Although he supported a modest work requirement for welfare recipients during the general election, he also proposed $6 billion in increased spending, including more money on the same sort of job training programs that have failed badly in the past. In contrast, New Jersey Governor James Florio, a liberal Democrat, lauded the reform bill as he signed it into law. The current system, he argued, is "corrupt," "morally bankrupt," and "entraps our children in a cradle-to-grave cycle of dependency."

Serious reform of the public welfare system, a frequent goal over the last three decades, has proved to be extremely difficult, but it would offer many benefits—not only an important source of budget savings, but also an opportunity to help break the debilitating cycle of dependency that has developed among many recipients. What the poor need more than anything else today is liberation from a system which ensnares and enfeebles them.

Yet the real answer is not likely to come from within the public sector. Unfortunately, the debate over welfare has itself been sadly impoverished. The conventional wisdom is that the only alternative to a government-run, taxpayer-financed system is private charity, an amalgam of idiosyncratic organizations and niggardly programs that would inevitably allow millions of needy to "fall through the cracks." Thus, the only "real" issues in the minds of most public officials involve what kind of government-run, taxpayer-financed system we should use:

universal or targeted, with an insurance element or not, and so on.

Yet the private alternative is not nearly so limited as is commonly conceived. Many different forms of social organizations have been used by different societies at different times to provide what is today called "welfare." In some societies, the extended family or kin group is the primary locus of providing a "safety net." In other cases, it comes through the church—the Mormons, for instance. Similarly, in Islamic society, welfare is financed by alms-giving, mandatory for Muslims, but the program is only organized rather than run by the state.

Perhaps the most interesting form of welfare institution in the West, at least to those concerned about individual liberty and personal independence, is collective self-help, or mutual aid, as it is more commonly called. Coexisting with traditional charity, mutual aid was the dominant form of welfare up into the 1920s in the U.S. and its international cousins, Australia, Britain, and Canada. Although fraternal societies were the main sources of such assistance, churches, community associations (represented by the "Community Chest" cards in Monopoly), labor unions, service institutions (such as hospitals, which raised money through contractual contributions), subscription societies, and temperance and self-improvement groups, also helped develop an extensive, yet voluntary, social network.

Not only was the plethora of mutual aid organizations effective and flexible, but the informal system had a positive moral impact, both on individuals and the larger culture. In particular, these groups embodied the principle of personal responsibility, self-help, and cooperative community action. These values, along with productive labor and thrift, were popular at the time, and were promoted in such books as Samuel Smiles's *Self Help* in Britain and Elbert Hubbard's *A Message to Garcia* in the U.S. Mutual aid as an institution highlighted the traditional distinction between deserving and undeserving poor, a difference further reflected in the practices and rules of most such organizations. Further, mutual aid was also essentially democratic and egalitarian, conflicting with both paternalism from state to citizen and from rich to poor.

Equally important, but little recognized today, mutual aid enhanced cooperation between unrelated individuals. Far from encouraging greed, selfishness, and isolation, mutual aid drew people into a system where responsibility for those in need was shared. Because the organizations were both smaller and more flexible than, say, the Department of Health and Human Services, their members necessarily had great involvement in the lives of those in need. The result was more of the real "compassion" that Olasky writes about, thereby encouraging independence, hard work, and self-respect among all parties. The existence of so many private aid institutions also played what many observers believe to be a major role in the "moralization" process in Britain and the U.S. during the 19th Century, a process that produced a 40-year decline in crime rates.

That mutual aid worked, and worked well, seems beyond dispute. This is why Charles Murray contends that many, if not most, of today's state welfare activities could be better performed by local and voluntary institutions. Yet an important question remains: why did this system decline so rapidly after the 1920s? The answer is important because it will help us determine whether or not it is possible to rely more on private social services in the future. In theory, at least, a welfare system based on a mixture of charitable institutions and mutual aid societies would best promote the values of interest to a classical liberal, especially freedom and responsibility, thereby fulfilling the only proper objectives for a welfare state. But is it possible to get from here to there? To the extent that the decline of mutual aid was linked to the severity of the Great Depression, for instance, it may be possible to revive such private entities today. The obvious change in the public's sense of individual and state responsibilities might be reversed by patient educational efforts. If the process is a result of modernity, or one or another particular institutional features of today's industrial society, however, then the chances for change seem much more dim.

Few people are satisfied with today's poverty programs, yet this element of the welfare state remains almost as sacrosanct politically as Social Security and other benefit programs. History provides us with numerous effective and voluntary alternatives to today's system, but, unfortunately, it gives us fewer lessons on how to gain popular acceptance for shifting the responsibility for welfare from the public to the private sector.

3. WHAT WENT WRONG WITH WELFARE: HOW OUR POVERTY PROGRAMS INJURED THE POOR

Michael Bauman

Michael Bauman, professor at Hillsdale College (MI), testifies with an original lament that seeks to narrate how we've failed in our poverty relief efforts. Bauman gives an easy lesson in economics and the fallacies of welfare disincentives, without preachments. His caveat is essential for any welfare reformer to take to heart prior to rebuilding. A beginning for reformation in welfare might be to admit that the present welfare system does often injure the poor, the opposite effect of its intention to show compassion.

> *Seeking to promote the welfare of the poor, the disadvantaged, the unemployed, and the misfortunate, well-meaning citizens—including a good many evangelical Christians—have inadvertently supported forms of economic organization that have promoted the precise outcomes they sought to alleviate. For too long, socially concerned Christians have measured policies by the intentions of their advocates, rather than the predictable effectiveness of the programs. Put simply, in our haste to do something constructive, we have not thought very seriously about the impact, particularly . . . , of alternative policies on the well-being of the intended beneficiaries.[1]*

*P*atty Newman has written: "Can you imagine my shock when I went into a welfare department and said, 'Do you mean to tell me that a woman can come in here every nine months and begin to get checks for another illegitimate child?' The welfare man said, 'Oh, no, Mrs. Newman, she has to claim a different man as father every time or else she doesn't get the money.' "

We thought we were doing the right thing. We thought that if we passed laws to raise their wages and lower their rent, if we gave generously to help support mothers without husbands and children without fathers, we could aid the poor in their flight from poverty and alleviate much of their distress while they were still in it. We were wrong.

We forgot that good intentions are not enough, and that virtually all government programs of any significant scope at all carry with them great loads of unintended consequences. We forgot that aiming is not hitting, and that meaning well is not doing well.

First, we thought that if we passed laws mandating higher wages for the lowest paid workers, we could increase their income and thereby aid the industrious poor in their escape from poverty. We forgot that the lowest paid workers were normally those with the least skill and the least experience, and that, in the marketplace, they are the least desirable of all workers. By artificially elevating their wages, we made them even more undesirable, making it increasingly unlikely they could ever get a job. This happened because we forgot that a wage is not merely a purchase price for an employer; it is a selling price for a worker. We passed laws preventing the least desirable workers from selling their services at a price their prospective employers, and ultimately the consumer, can afford to pay.

If you have little or no skill and experience, and yet the government requires you to sell your services at an artificially inflated price, you will not find anyone to purchase them because, in order to pay for your overpriced services, your employer must raise his own selling price. In turn, this means that your employer is increasingly likely to go out of business and that all his current employees, who are more skilled than you, more experienced than you, and worth the money he pays them, lose their jobs because those companies who were wise enough not to hire you at the legally mandated price can produce the same product your company produces, but at a lower cost both to themselves and to their customers. We forgot that all workers work not merely for their employer, but also for the consumer, and that consumers wisely try to make the most of their money. Your product, because of its bloated cost of production, remains on the shelf or in the warehouse. In short, we passed laws requiring employers to pay higher wages to their least desirable workers while, as good stewards of the resources God has given us, we wisely elected not to buy the overpriced products of those who do as the law demands, thereby putting them out of business, which creates more unemployed workers and more poor, whom we then try to help with minimum wage laws.

Perhaps the point can be made more graphically at the corporate level. Imagine that, in an effort to aid portions of our lagging auto industry, we decided to prop up the profits of our weakest car maker by passing a law that put a minimum price of $25,000 on each vehicle it sold, thus dramatically increasing the profits it enjoyed from every sale. But, despite our good intention, indeed because of it, that auto maker soon goes out of business because, no matter how much they want to "buy American," very few consumers willingly pay that much money for cars comparable to those available elsewhere for half the price. The same principle holds when that which is being sold is not a car, but an unskilled employee's overpriced labor. To such harmful, but well intentioned, legislative conniving, no thinking Christian ought to consent.

Instead, as economist Charles Van Eaton has carefully argued, we ought to encourage more entrepreneurship like that of marketplace giants Ray Kroc or Dave Thomas, who, far more than any government program ever has or could, aided the cause of the poor, both as consumers and as workers. Kroc and Thomas aided the poor as consumers by providing low-income workers with inexpensive ways to treat their hard working spouses and their underprivileged children to enjoyable meals outside the home, a privilege reserved largely for the prosperous before the advent of fast food restaurants.

Even now, decades after the inception of McDonald's, children twitter with excitement at the prospect of a cheeseburger, fries, and a Coke, much like their mothers, who are spared the drudgery of cooking yet another meal and cleaning yet another load of dirty dishes. Kroc and Thomas aided impoverished workers by providing the all-important entry-level jobs, by which unskilled or inexperienced workers could learn critical marketplace lessons concerning the importance of appearance, punctuality, deference, teamwork, and dependability; jobs by which they could acquire management and public relations skills; jobs by which they could acquire the personal references and endorsements necessary to obtain better jobs with other employers in the future, and jobs by which they could earn a modest wage to boot.

Kroc and Thomas did more to aid the poor than does the state because Kroc and Thomas understood that you cannot climb the ladder of success without first getting on the ladder. Kroc and Thomas invited the poor to step onto the first rung, and made it possible for them to do so. Untold thousands of people prospered in precisely this way, all without spending even one tax dollar. Quite the opposite, in fact, for these novice workers themselves, as they rose from poverty, actually paid into public coffers. In fact, nearly 10 percent of the entire American work force has worked for Kroc or Thomas at one time or another. Because of people like Kroc and Thomas, great numbers of minority poor became wealthy franchisees, many even owning entire chains of franchises. Thousands more gained access to management

jobs that otherwise would have remained perpetually un-
attainable.

Second, we thought that if we passed laws holding
down the costs of urban housing, we could aid the poor
by making many more thousands of inexpensive apartments available to them than before, and perhaps diminish homelessness in the process. We forgot that a
purchase price for a renter is a selling price for a land-
lord. The more attractive a price is for the one, the less
attractive it is for the other. When landlords are forced to
reduce their rents in the face of burgeoning tax and maintenance costs, they wisely decide to allocate their very
substantial investments in other ways. For example,
when rent-control ceilings make it unprofitable for landlords to rent their apartments, they often sell those apartments as condominiums, and thus escape real estate taxes
and the high cost of urban upkeep, not to mention make
enough money to send junior and his sister to a better
college than they otherwise could attend. Because the
supply of condominiums then increases, their selling
price tends to go down, thereby aiding wealthy urban
dwellers, the only ones who can afford to purchase them.
Meanwhile, the price of the apartments still on the market now rises because their supply has shrunk. By trying
to control rent in order to aid the poor, we aid the
wealthy by driving down the price of their housing, and
we injure those in poverty by decreasing the number of
apartments available for them to rent at any price, driving more of them onto the street.

In order to prevent this dire consequence, we sometimes pass laws prohibiting landlords from taking re-
course to condominium conversion. This legislation
predictably proves counterproductive because it often
means, first, that landlords seek additional payments un-

der the table from their renters, thus making life more difficult for the poor, who can scarcely afford the extra cost; second, that landlords defer needed maintenance on their decaying buildings, again making life more difficult for the poor; and third, that landlords get out of the housing business altogether, tear down their apartments, and build a parking lot—a low maintenance, high yield investment that serves only those wealthy enough to afford the high cost of owning, operating, and insuring an automobile in an urban setting.

We must remember that, human nature being what it is, people respond to incentives. Therefore, rather than passing rent-control laws, we ought to give significantly reduced utility rates and impressive tax breaks to those who create, or who maintain, urban rental housing, thus making such housing more plentiful and more affordable. In short, we should do all we can to promote the supply side of the supply and demand equation. The greater the supply, the lower the price. The lower the price, the better it is for the poor. The greater the incentives for property owners, the better it is for landlords. The better it is for landlords, the greater the supply of apartments. Furthermore, the increase in urban rental units not only results in lower rental prices for renters, it also provides more jobs for those who construct apartment buildings, as well as for those who service them and who maintain them.

To that sort of plan, a conscientious Christian can consent.

Third, we thought that by transferring money as generously as we could afford to the mothers of illegitimate children, we could soften the pains of kids without fathers and of mothers without husbands. We forgot what insurance companies often call "moral hazard," which is insuring against a disaster in such a way as to actually cause the misfortune in question. That is, insurance companies know that because people follow incentives, if an insurance policy pays off too handsomely, calamity occurs. If the fire insurance policy on a floundering business pays more money to the owner than the owner can get from operating the business, that business is likely to burn. The temptation seems sometimes too great to resist. Likewise, if a life insurance policy pays off so lucratively that the insured's beneficiaries are better off if the insured is dead, death sometimes results. If medical insurance covers too great a portion of medical expenses, people tend to go for treatment of illnesses that are hardly illnesses at all, thus tying up doctors, clinics, hospitals, and pharmacies with cases that too often are trivial. In other words, when you reach the point of moral hazard, fire insurance causes fires, life insurance causes death, and medical insurance causes illness. Not surprisingly, insurance companies try hard always to avoid the moral hazard inherent in insurance. They learned the hard way that the threshold of moral hazard is reached very quickly.

Our governmental approaches to welfare have not.

In our rush to do well for households without a male breadwinner, we forgot that welfare is poverty insurance and, as result, we actually helped cause the problem we were intending to alleviate. As the epigraph from Patty Newman that heads this essay indicates, by making illegitimate children a credential for increased financial support, we made certain more illegitimate children were born. Tragically, however, the more illegitimate children a woman has, the more deeply she becomes mired in poverty, and the less likely it becomes that she can ever extricate herself from it, despite the money she is given. As is all too clear, poverty circles around single parent homes, especially when the single parent is a woman. But single motherhood is what we decided to pay for, and it is what we got. As one noted policy analyst observed, this is an incentive program from hell.

Put another way, in our effort to aid single mothers and their children, we made low-income husbands extraneous. We sent the signal to many thousands of young women, young women eager to get out of their parents' home and out of their parents' control, that poor men are most useful to poor women as procreators, not providers. That signal was clearly and widely received.

To poor young men that same signal had a different but equally devastating effect, for it served to detach their actions from those actions' attendant consequences. We taught those young men that, if they wanted it, sex was a game they could play for free. No longer was there heavy pressure upon them to face up to the many unfortunate consequences of sex outside of marriage. No longer did young men feel compelled to work long hours at difficult jobs in order to provide food, clothing, and shelter for the new lives they were creating or for the financially dependent women who helped create them. That tab, they soon learned, could be picked up by their rich Uncle Sam, who worked in government. With no compelling need to channel time and energy into acquiring useful skills and into applying those skills profitably in the marketplace, increasing numbers of poor young men simply took to the streets, where life got boring and then got worse, much worse.

In our misguided efforts to be good Samaritans, to help those lying in the ditch of poverty, we forgot that whatever undermines traditional family values, roles, and ties, undermines society itself. To such moral and social degeneration, no consistent Christian desires to subscribe.

Fourth, by giving money to the poor, we thought we were simply aiding and comforting the unfortunate in their time of difficulty. We forgot that giving good gifts is an exceedingly difficult endeavor and that poverty is not always itself the problem; it is often the symptom of another prior problem. That is, if poverty (the lack of money) really was what ails the poor, supplying vast amounts of money would surely alleviate it. After nearly thirty years of Great Society-like welfare programs, however, programs that transferred countless billions—yes, billions—of dollars to the poor, poverty is still winning the war we wage against it.

We forgot that of the many reasons why people are poor, only a few lie outside their own control. We did not tell them that the surest way to get ahead in modern America is precisely the way people have done it for decades: get a good education (which includes both a mastery of English and of computation), work harder than those above you, save money, and invest it. We told them, instead, that in order to get more money they needed to demand it from government, not to earn it in the marketplace, as if financial improvement were a public entitlement, not a private achievement, and as if they were incapable of succeeding by the same means countless other Americans had employed in the past.

Then, apparently in an effort to allay some of the responsibility the poor themselves have to make their own lives better, and to lighten the burden that such responsibility inevitably entails, we told them that they were poor because the wealthy oppressed them. In other words, we taught the poor to blame their poverty on prejudice.

In a perverse sort of way, we were right about the connection between prejudice and poverty. Indeed, prejudice *does* lead to poverty, though not in the way we expected. We convinced the poor that the prosperous prosper only at someone else's expense and usually by deceit and because of greed. Not only are such insulting generalizations not true about the wealthy and instances of bearing false witness against our neighbors, they are crippling to the poor. If a poor man believes that the wealthy are exploitive thieves who squash other people into poverty for their own gain, that impoverished man will not likely climb the ladder of economic success. Impoverished man remains poor for two reasons: first, he no longer respects either those above him or their achievement, thus making it far less likely that he will seek to emulate them; and second, he becomes blind to the path the wealthy actually take to success—hard work, sacrifice, postponed gratification, and diligence.

At our hands the poor were too easily convinced that they were poor primarily because of reasons which they could not change and over which they had no control. We taught the poor to be prejudiced themselves—prejudiced against the prosperous. That prejudice proved morally and economically debilitating. We blamed poverty on prejudice and then promoted prejudice among the poor. In the wake of that false and crippling bias, too many of them simply gave up. We forgot not only that ideas have consequences, but that bad ideas have bad ones.

We also forgot to tie our charity more securely to the sincere efforts of the recipient. We mistakenly decided to give aid to the poor, not to *the deserving and industrious poor,* that is, to those who are poor through no fault of their own, or whose escape from poverty can never be produced by their own efforts. In doing so, we ignored St. Paul's prudent Scriptural principle: if a man will not work, he shall not eat (II Thess. 3:10). We should have remembered that love does not squander either its resources or itself in reckless disregard of people's character and actions. By obliterating the distinction between the deserving and the undeserving poor, we ran contrary to the will and practice of God, who treats the undeserving poor as objects, not of mercy but of wrath.

In other words, we forgot that real love helps those who cannot help themselves. It refuses to subsidize sluggardliness or indolence by doing for others what they can and ought to do on their own. Christian love operates upon the premise that the defeat of poverty is a joint effort, or common endeavor, between the haves and the have nots, not a unilateral thrust by the haves only. The recipients of Christian charity ought to be either diligent workers or else unable. The unwilling and the slothful must get nothing from us but exhortation. To give something else is to do them moral injury, something Christian love does not do.

As long as we fail to distinguish between the deserving and the undeserving poor, we teach others that poverty is an entitlement and that the blessings of life and labor are yours for the asking or for the demanding, regardless of your contribution.

Finally, in this regard, our indiscriminate giving created a culture of dependence, one in which the connection between effort and prosperity was severed. By failing to distinguish the deserving poor from the undeserving, we told the economically disadvantaged that the diligent application of their private means to the alleviation of their personal distress is either unimportant or ineffective. This misconception implies that if the impoverished are ever to escape poverty it can only be by someone else's doing. This message, coupled with the notion that the poor are poor because of the perverse machinations of the rich, leads the poor to conclude that they are not responsible either for their poverty or their extrication from it. By sparing the poor the challenge of their own success, we consign them to state-funded dependency. We lead them in a direction quite the opposite of that articulated in John Kennedy's memorable challenge: "Ask not what your country can do for you."

Thus, while paternalism prospers, the poor do not. On many fronts and in many ways, our poverty programs have failed to reduce poverty. What is worse, they have sometimes injured the very people they were designed to aid. Much of the blame is ours.

4. STATISM: LAND OF THE FREE?

R. C. Sproul and R. C. Sproul, Jr.

In this short essay by theologians R. C. Sproul and R. C. Sproul, Jr. the underlying culprit of our welfare abyss is identified as statism. The insightful Bible teachers from Ligonier Ministries comment on the attitudes of dependency which have been created by ill-founded statist expectations in modern welfare. Their suggestion is that we first have a clearer and more Biblically grounded view of the state's proper role before we overlay that with welfare policies.

Another cornerstone is affirming individual responsibility. The most serious problems plaguing the black underclass have to do with a breakdown of the family. Too many young black children are being raised without the presence of good men in their lives. How do we begin to reverse this fact? By crafting economic and social policies that support the two-parent family; fashioning public policies that reward right behavior and penalize wrong behavior; using all the means at our disposal—in our public, private, and social spheres, through law and moral suasion—to condemn irresponsible acts (for example, fathering children and not supporting them); putting young men in the presence of positive male role models; and insisting that people in responsible positions affirm the right things (honoring commitments, individual responsibility, hard work, community norms, and virtue, to name a few). Some of the solutions involve government action. Many do not.[1]

A number of years ago I shared a taxi with Francis Schaeffer in St. Louis. During our cab ride I asked Dr. Schaeffer, "What is your greatest concern for the future of America?" Without hesitation or interval given to pondering the question, Schaeffer replied simply, "Statism."

What did Schaeffer mean? What was at the heart of his concern? To answer these questions, we need a clear understanding of statism. Our understanding of the term is often obfuscated by a tendency to think of statism as a phenomenon that only exists in autocratic totalitarian governments. We tend to associate it with dictatorships, not with democracies.

Upon closer scrutiny we realize that statism, as an *ism,* can function within the structure of any form of government, be it a monarchy, an oligarchy, a democracy, or a dictatorship. Statism is chiefly a philosophy, an ideology that attends one's view of government. The philosophy usually yields certain results that culminate in tyranny, but the results must not be confused with the philosophy.

Statism involves a philosophy of government by which the state, or government, is viewed not only as the final ruling authority but the ultimate agency of redemption. In this sense the state does not simply coexist with the church. It supplants the church. Statism can never function *under God.* If the state is deemed to be under God in the sense of being under God's authority and accountable to God for its actions, then the state cannot be the ultimate authority.

In the philosophy of statism, the government is conceived of as *autonomous.* It may take shape in an autonomous king, an autonomous dictator, an autonomous committee, or even in an autonomous democratic populous.

The classical safeguard against autonomous government is the concept of law, which is usually embodied in some form of constitution. The Greek word for law is *nomos.* To be autonomous means to be a law unto oneself (autonomy = self-law).

Herein lies the essential difference between a constitutional monarchy and an absolute monarchy, or the difference between a *republic* and a *democracy.* In a pure democracy, the ultimate authority rests with the will of the majority. Here the majority rule of the people gives autonomy to the majority over the minority or the individual. There is no higher authority than the majority vote. In this view the people's autonomy is expressed by their representative government. A government by the people, of the people, and for the people can be statist. It allows for the possibility of a tyranny of the majority over minorities and individuals, as the Frenchman Alexis de Toqueville warned.

In a republic, the authority rests with the law. The classic formula for a republic is *Rule by law, not rule by men.* The purpose of a constitution is to establish inalienable rights protected by law. Such laws are designed to guarantee certain rights to minorities and individuals. In practical terms this means that an individual's rights cannot be taken away by the simple vote of a majority. This is what the civil rights battle was all about.

If, for example, one hundred Americans in a given community vote to prohibit one person's expression of religion or speech, the individual can appeal to the First Amendment to protect his rights against the will of the majority. In pure statism the rights of individuals are swallowed up by the state. Law does not rule. Rulers rule and rule autonomously.

The second critical idea of statism is that the state supplants the church as the chief instrument of redemption. People look to the state, not to God, for *salvation.* That Marx consciously developed such a view is well documented. For him the eschatological agent of redemption was the state.

While I was writing this article, the city of Los Angeles was burning, and sociologists, historians, and psychologists were musing on the causes for the 1992 riots. Once the first Rodney King trial ended in the jury's acquittal of the L.A. police officers, the city exploded in violence, resulting in untold millions of dollars in property damage, hundreds of fires, hundreds wounded, and scores left dead.

The question we ask is, why? Certainly the contributing factors are many and complex. One of those factors, which will probably be overlooked, involves the people's reaction to the state. On the one hand, the riots may be viewed as a reaction *against* statism. The uprising in Tiananmen Square in China and the myriad of uprisings in the Soviet Bloc that led to the disintegration of the Soviet Union may all be viewed as violent protests against statism. In Los Angeles, people were enraged against the state because they believed Rodney King's rights were violated. They perceived that the state failed to uphold the law. The irony is that their response was an act of unbridled lawlessness. Angered by the state's disregard for the law, they took to the streets to protest by radically violating their neighbors' rights. They burned, they looted, they beat, and they shot their neighbors with a savagery that far exceeded what King himself endured.

What is astonishing about all this was the attitude some of the looters expressed. One, interviewed on CNN, was asked, "Why did you take that television set from the store?" He replied, "It was free." The assumption of some of the looters was one of entitlement. It was a thinly veiled protest against the state's promise of redemption via proliferating entitlements. The state had failed to *deliver the goods,* so they simply helped themselves to the goods.

In this sense, and to this degree, the riots in Los Angeles were not so much a protest against statism, but a result of the myth of statism. It was a demand for *more* statism.

Democratic statism lives by the myth of state redemption. The dream is that the state will provide all my needs. It will provide food for my table, education for my children, money for my bank account, employment for my career, and a host of other benefits that will cover me from the cradle to the grave. Welfare founded on statism is and will be a failure.

Too many recipients of statism begin with *appreciation* for such provisions, move quickly to an *expectation* of these provisions, and then finally to a *demand* for these provisions. If the demand is not met, they take to the streets like children throwing temper tantrums.

I call the dream of statist redemption a myth because it cannot become a reality. The dream quickly becomes a nightmare. The size of government increases geometrically as more and more demands are placed upon it. The power of government increases geometrically as more hope is invested in it. Finally the cost of government increases geometrically as the price tag for the provisions escalates. While all this happens, the ability of government to function diminishes geometrically as it builds bigger and bigger deficits and drains more and more of the nation's resources. Its laws become confused and contradictory, its operation becomes unwieldy and paralyzed, and its excellence diminishes with the diminished quality of its leaders.

The United States began as an experiment in liberty. The guiding principle that underpinned the Union was *that which governs least, governs best*. The idea of freedom took a fundamental shift in the eighteenth century. Prior to that, a nation was considered to be free if no foreign nation ruled over her. The Enlightenment ushered in the idea that freedom required no government interference in a man's life. This meant autocracy, or self-rule.

The Declaration of Independence deposed government by declaring that men's rights come not from the state but from the Creator. The Constitution and the Bill of Rights established inviolable boundaries over which government was forbidden to cross. From this rich soil of freedom, America blossomed.

This concept remained fixed for more than a century and a half. It was poked, prodded, and pricked here and there, but Americans retained, by and large, their self-reliance. Yet the door of change creaked open when America plunged into a world war and the Great Depression. Franklin Delano Roosevelt spoke of freedom, but its meaning shifted. Roosevelt did not mean freedom from governmental intrusion but *freedom from fear* and *freedom from want*. This type of freedom required more government. After the decades of calamity that preceded Roosevelt's presidency and with turmoil brewing in Europe, the American people accepted this hollow freedom as their savior.

Government then became the solution rather than the problem. Once it had the American people secure inside its gilded cage, the state was free to grow virtually at will. How large has this leviathan become? One standard of measurement is the size of government employment. In the early part of the twentieth century, all levels of government—federal, state, and local—employed approximately 4 percent of the civilian labor force. In 1950, the government employed about 10 percent of the labor force. Now, the level has escalated to approximately 14 percent; one out of every seven workers is employed by the government. These figures do not include the nearly two million members of the armed forces or civilians engaged in quasi-government service, such as the employees of defense contractors.

Perhaps a better measure of the size of government is the percentage of the gross national product consumed by the state. Early in this century, all levels of government took in 6 to 7 percent of the GNP. By 1950, revenues had reached 24 percent of the GNP. Currently, that rate stands at 32 percent. This statistic alone does not do justice to the problem. Properly interpreted, this means that of the fruit of labor produced annually by every person in the country, the government consumes nearly one-third.[2]

Such is the cost of our brave new world. Where once we cherished self-reliance, now we turn to the state with all our woes. Government-funded hospitals (or whatever new national healthcare program the government creates) ensure Junior is born safely. Food stamps and Aid to Families with Dependent Children feed Junior as he grows. Governmental childcare watches over Junior while his parents work. The public schools train, indoctrinate, and feed Junior. Government loans and grants pay Junior's tuition at the state university. The state employment agency finds Junior a job. Should he tire of working, the government will gladly send his unemployment check. The Federal Housing Administration will prop up Junior's credit so he can buy a house (and the Federal Reserve will ensure easy money to keep the economy growing). The same process will apply to Junior's children until Junior is ready to retire. Social Security will buy his groceries, and Medicare will meet his health-care needs. Cradle to the grave, Junior lives in a gilded cage— every need met, every responsibility denied.

Long vigilant against the communist menace, we have allowed the state to ensnare us from within. While we manned the ramparts against *1984,* a *Brave New World* overtook us. Our fear of the future and our love of comfort continually drive us to forsake freedom. We

have failed to heed the warning from one founding father, Benjamin Franklin: "Those who would give up essential liberty to purchase a little temporary safety
deserve neither liberty nor safety."

As long as the statist philosophy—or more accurately,
mythology—persists, the nation languishes. The people
become like the proverbial frog which is boiled alive
while the water heats so gradually that by the time the
frog realizes he's in hot water, it's too late to jump out.

During the recession, the nation faced high unemployment. Those unemployed demanded more unemployment benefits, which placed more strain on the
budget, more tax burden on the people and on businesses, and resulted in more unemployment . . . and the
beat goes on as the myth refuses to die.

Meanwhile, Francis Schaeffer enjoys the final refuge
from statism as he beholds the reality of his own redemption.[3]

Part II

WELFARE REFORMED: BIBLICAL PRINCIPLES

5. THREE ESSENTIAL ELEMENTS OF BIBLICAL CHARITY: FAITH, FAMILY, AND WORK

George Grant

Prolific author and esteemed Christian leader George Grant, Executive Director of The Christian Worldview Institute, with typical flair and perception gives readers one of the best summary statements of what will work in welfare reform. He urges policy formulators to elevate to prominence these three essential values—a lively faith, value-generating families, and a work ethic— each drawn from Scripture. A reformation of welfare must return to these.

> *I hasten to add that a charity which knows*
> *how to give only money and not also itself is*
> *not yet the Christian love. Then alone will*
> *you be justified when you also offer your*
> *time, your ability and the sympathy of your*
> *inventiveness to help end such injustices for*
> *all time, and when you let nothing hidden in*
> *the treasure house of your Christian religion*
> *remain un-utilized against the cancer which*
> *is destroying the dynamic of our society in*
> *such disturbing ways.*[1]

*L*ike honoring our parents, caring for the poor is a command with a promise. The Bible tells us that if we would uphold the mandate to be generous to the poor, we would ourselves be happy (Pr. 14:21); God would preserve us (Ps. 41:1–2); we would prosper and be satisfied (Pr. 11:25); and we would be raised up from beds of affliction (Ps. 41:3). Thus it has always been the aspiration of the faithful to be "zealous of good works" (Titus 2:14 KJV).

At a time when any and all other Christian virtues have been utterly abandoned, this one—caring for the needy—still remains. We are all agreed that charity is a good thing. Unfortunately, though, because charity remains in isolation, its good intentioned naivete may cause more harm than good. As a good out of its place, it has at times ceased to be good.

Charles Haddon Spurgeon has said, "They say you may praise a fool till you make him useful: I don't know much about that, but I do know that if I get a bad knife I generally cut my finger, and a blunt axe is far more trouble than profit. A handsaw is a good thing—but not to shave with. A pig's tail will never make a good arrow; nor will his ear make a silk purse. You can't catch rabbits with drums or pigeons with plums. A good thing is not good out of its place."

The purpose of this essay is not to establish that charity is a good thing. But rather to establish its place. It is to contend that without at least three essential ingredients—providing charity with its appropriate context—it becomes as useless and as uncomfortable as shaving with a handsaw.

Faith

The first essential element of Biblical charity is *faith*. What a person thinks, what he believes, what shapes his ultimate concerns, and what he holds to be true in his heart—in other words, his faith or lack of it—has a direct effect on his material well-being. And it has a direct effect on whether or not he can alter that well-being. "For as [a man] thinketh in his heart, so is he" (Pr. 23:7 KJV).

In 1905, Max Weber, the renowned political economist and "founding father" of sociology, affirmed this fundamental truth for modern social scientists in his classic *The Protestant Ethic and the Spirit of Capitalism*. He argued that the remarkable prosperity of the West was directly attributable to the cultural, personal, and ethical prevalence of the Christian faith. In contrast to pagan cultures, where freedoms and opportunities were severely limited and where poverty and suffering abounded, Weber found that commitment to definite religious tenets brought men and nations both liberty and prosperity.

According to the Bible, the reasons for this are multi-tudinous.

First, the Christian faith reorients fallen men to reality. Because of sin we are naturally blind (2 Pet. 1:9), foolish (Tit. 3:3), ignorant (Isa. 56:10), and self-destructive (Pr. 24:2). We are ruled by our passions (Jas. 5:17), our lusts (Jas. 1:14), and our delusions (Isa. 53:6).

"Men without faith in the Savior," said the great Puritan divine Richard Baxter, "are damned to rootless lives of fantasy, frustration, and failure. For indeed, apart from the Light of His Life, all men must needs be ever in darkness." The poor need Jesus Christ. They need the "Bread of Life" (Jn. 6:48–51). The ultimate poverty engendering perpetual deprivation is a lack of faith.

Second, the Christian faith counteracts the destructive effects of sin. Sin is not a concept that has much currency with the modern social scientists, economists, politicians, community organizers, civil rights activists, and social service providers that administer our government's programs for the poor. That bankruptcy may account for their utter and dismal failure.

Sin is, in fact, one of the chief causes of poverty. Surely injustice (Is. 58:6), calamity (Gen. 47:13–19), famine (Lev. 25:25, 39, 47), and exploitation (Jas. 5:1–2) cause poverty, and Christians must meet those causes and that poverty with unmitigated mercy (2 Cor. 8:1–15). But we must realize as well that a vast amount of poverty is self-inflicted. Men who do not know Christ and do not walk in faith are more often than not immoral, impure, and improvident (Gal. 5:19–21). They are prone to extreme and destructive behavior, indulging in perverse vices and dissipating sensuality (1 Cor. 6:9–10). And they are thus driven over the brink of poverty (Pr. 23:21).

On the other hand, "if any man be in Christ, he is a new creature: the old things are passed away; behold, all things are become new" (2 Cor. 5:17 KJV). The Christian faith reforms sinners with new and constructive values. We are provoked to moral and upright lives of diligence, purity, sober-mindedness, thrift, trustworthiness, and responsibility (Col. 3:5–15). Where poverty germinates in the rotting soil of sin, productivity flourishes in the fertile field of faith.

Third, the Christian faith establishes a future orientation in men. All too often the poor either flounder in a dismal fatalism or they squander their few resources in an irresponsible impulsiveness. They are short-sighted (Pr. 6:6–11), unmotivated (Pr. 28:19), and naive (Pr. 7:6–23). And "where there is no vision, the people perish" (Pr. 29:18).

The Christian faith teaches men to live thoughtfully (Mt. 25:13–30), to plan (Mt. 7:24–27), to exercise restraint (Eph. 4:25–32), and to defer gratification in order to achieve higher ends (Jas. 5:7). We are provoked to self-control (Gal. 5:22–23), wisdom (Jas. 3:13–17), and careful stewardship in order to build for the future (Gen. 1:28). According to Thrasymachos of Trace, a fifth-century Church historian, "Christless lives are goalless lives. And goalless lives are wealthless lives." In order to break the yoke of poverty we must invade the culture of the moment with the dynamic escalation of Christ.

Fourth, the Christian faith provokes men to exercise responsibility. Outside the grace of salvation and sanctification men are naturally prone to selfishness, wastefulness, and sloth (2 Pet. 2:2–3).

In Christ, though, men grow into selfless maturity (Phil. 2:3–4). We are responsible to redeem our time

(Eph. 5:16). We are responsible to make the most of every opportunity (Col. 4:5). We are responsible to fulfill our calling in life (1 Pet. 4:10). We are responsible to use our money wisely (Dt. 8:18), to care for our families (1 Tim. 5:8), to serve the needs of others (Lk. 22:25–30), and to be an example of redemption before all men (1 Pet. 3:1–17). It is this very kind of diligent responsibility—this very fruit of faith—that the poor most need if they are ever to climb out of the broken cistern of dispossession.

Fifth, the Christian faith empowers men with confidence in the "very great and precious promises of God" (2 Pet. 1:3–4). God blesses obedience (Dt. 28:1–14). He curses wickedness (Dt. 28:15–68). So even though every believer suffers through life's normal setbacks, struggles, sicknesses, and strife, we have the assurance that in the end God's sovereign hand will set it all aright (Rom. 8:28). We can confidently claim the magnificent benefits of the covenant (Heb. 4:16). We can appropriate the glorious riches of the heavenly realm (Eph. 1:3).

The poor need God's blessing. They need the rewards of His favor. But "without faith it is impossible to please God, because anyone who comes to him must believe that he exists, and that he rewards those who earnestly seek him" (Heb. 11:6).

If Biblical charity is a genuine attempt to transform poverty into productivity, its agenda will necessarily include discipleship in the essentials of the Christian faith—beginning with soteriology and carrying on through to complete maturity. Neither a transfer of wealth, nor a massive reeducation agenda, nor an impenetrable economic safety net, nor a comprehensive social welfare program, nor all of these things together, can substitute for this. "It is faith," says George Gilder, "in all its multifarious forms and luminosities, that can by itself move the mountains of sloth and depression that afflict the world's stagnant economies; it brought immigrants thousands of miles with pennies in their pockets to launch the American empire of commerce; and it performs miracles daily in our present impasse."

Authentic Christianity goes to work equipping the poor to walk in faith. That's Biblical charity.

Family

The second essential element of Biblical charity is *family*.

The family is the basic building block of society. When the family begins to break down, the rest of society begins to disintegrate. This is particularly evident in the lives of the poor. A full 75 percent of those living below the poverty line in this country live in broken homes. In times of economic calamity, intact families are ten times more likely to recover and ultimately prosper than broken families.

There is no replacement for the family. The government can't substitute services for it. Social workers can't substitute kindness and understanding for it. Educators can't substitute knowledge, skills, or facilitation for it. The poor need the family. They need fathers, and mothers, and brothers, and sisters. They need grandparents, and aunts, and uncles, and cousins. "There is no other place," wrote John Chrysostom in the fourth century, "where the human spirit can be so nurtured as to prosper spiritually, intellectually, and temporally, than in the bosom of the family's rightful relation."

There are several reasons for this.

First, family life provides men with a proper sense of identity. In the midst of our families we can know and be

known. We can taste the joys and sorrows of genuine
intimacy. We can gain a vision of life that is sober and
sure. We are bolstered by the love of family (Lk. 11:11–
13). We are strengthened by the confidence of family
(Jn. 1:39–42). We are emboldened by the legacy of family (Gen. 49:3–27). And we are stabilized by the objec-
tivity of family (Heb. 12:7–11). The poor desperately
need this kind of perspective. They desperately need to
be stabilized in the gentle environs of hearth and home.

Second, family life provides men with a genuine social security. There's no place like home. In times of
trouble our greatest resource will always be those who
know us best and love us most. Because family members
share a common sense of destiny with one another and a
bond of intimacy to one another they can—and will—
rush to one another's sides when needed. And well they
should. That is just as God intended it (1 Tim. 5:8).

"Caesars and Satraps attempt to succor our wounds
and wants with opulent circuses and eloquent promises,"
said Methodius, the famed seventh-century missionary to
the Slavs. "All such dolations are mere pretense, however, in comparison to the genuine Christian care afforded at even the coarsest family hearth."

Third, family life provides men with the accountability
and discipline they need. Families are an incubator for
sound values (Dt. 6:4–9). They reinforce the principles of
authority (1 Pet. 3:1–7), structure (Eph. 5:22–33), liability
(Heb. 12:7–11), obedience (Eph. 6:1–9), and selflessness
(Eph. 5:21). According to economist Michael Novak,
family accountability and discipline bring out the very
best in us. He says, "A typical mother or father without
thinking twice about it would willingly die—in a fire or
accident, say—in order to save one of his or her children.

While in most circumstances this human act would be regarded as heroic, for parents it is only ordinary. Thus . . . the Creator has shaped family life to teach as a matter of course the role of virtue."

If the poor are to be equipped in any measure to rise up from their beds of affliction, prisons of addiction, and ghettos of restriction, then Biblical charity must retrain them in the fine art of family living. It must be the aim of Biblical charity to strengthen marriages, equip parents, encourage intimacy, and heal brokenness.

Authentic Christianity goes to work establishing the poor in stable families. That's Biblical charity.

Work

The third essential element of Biblical charity is *work*.

Work is the heart and soul, the cornerstone, of Biblical charity. In fact, much of the outworking of Biblical charity is little more than a subfunction of the doctrine of work. Its operating resources are the fruit of work: the tithe, hospitality, private initiative, and voluntary relief. Its basic methodologies are rooted in the work ethic: gleaning, training, lending, and facilitating. Its primary objectives revolve around a comprehension of the goodness of work: productivity, rehabilitation, and entrepreneurial effect.

This is because work is the heart and soul, the cornerstone, of man's created purpose. God's first Word to man was definitive: "Be fruitful and increase in number; fill the earth and subdue it. Rule over the fish of the sea and the birds of the air and over every living creature that moves on the ground" (Gen. 1:28). In other words, work.

Throughout Scripture this emphasis is not only maintained, it is amplified: "Ill-gotten treasures are of no value, but righteousness delivers from death. The Lord does not let the righteous go hungry but he thwarts the craving of the wicked. Lazy hands make a man poor, but diligent hands bring wealth" (Pr. 10:2–4). "The sluggard craves and gets nothing, but the desires of the diligent are fully satisfied. . . . Dishonest money dwindles away, but he who gathers money [by labor, KJV] little by little makes it grow" (Pr. 13:4, 11).

The Bible is replete with teaching on work. But its basic thrust may be fairly reduced to four points.

First, the Bible teaches that all honorable work is holy. "A man can do nothing better than to . . . find satisfaction in his work" (Eccl. 2:24; 3:22). Far from being a bitter consequence of the Fall, work is a vital aspect of God's overall purpose for man in space and time. For that reason, He has typically used workmen, ordinary laborers, in the enactment of that purpose. He has used shepherds like Jacob and David. He has used farmers like Amos and Gideon. He has used merchants like Abraham and Lydia. He has used artists like Solomon and Bezalel. And the men He chose to revolutionize the Roman Empire in the first century were a motley band of fishermen and tax collectors. The great Puritan, Hugh Latimer, best captured the Biblical emphasis on the holiness of man's work when he wrote, "Our Savior, Christ Jesus, was a carpenter and got His living with great labor. Therefore, let no man disdain . . . to follow Him in a . . . common calling and occupation."

The Fourth Commandment, though commonly and correctly understood as prohibition against working on the Sabbath, has another all-too-often neglected injunction: "Six days you shall labor and do all your work" (Ex. 20:9). Richard Steele, another of the great Puritans, could confidently expect the presence and blessing of God: "Work is holy unto the Lord, ordained by His immutable Way." Everyone, even the partially disabled, reaps honor from industrious, productive work.

Second, the Bible teaches that God calls each person to his or her work. "There are different kinds of gifts, but the same Spirit. There are different kinds of service, but the same Lord. There are different kinds of working, but the same God works all of them in all men" (1 Cor. 12:4–6). The doctrine of calling was once the cornerstone of the Reformation. And rightly so. As Martin Luther wrote long ago, "The world does not consider labor a blessing, therefore, it flees and hates it . . . but the pious who fear the Lord labor with a ready and cheerful heart; for they know God's command and will, they acknowledge His calling."

Similarly, Cotton Mather, the great American colonial preacher, wrote, "A Christian should follow his occupation with contentment. . . . Is your business here clogged with any difficulties and inconveniences? Contentment under those difficulties is no little part of your homage to that King who hath placed you where you are by His call." William Tyndale also wrote, "If we look externally there is a difference betwixt the washing of dishes and preaching of the Word of God; but as touching to please God, in relation to His call, none at all."

Third, the Bible teaches that work is intended for the benefit of the community. It is not just to benefit ourselves. By work, we are to uphold our responsibility to provide for our family (1 Tim. 5:8), and build the work of Christ's Kingdom (Dt. 8:18), and share with those in need (Eph. 4:28). As John Calvin so aptly asserted, "We know that all men were created to busy themselves with labor . . . for the

common good." And Martin Luther wrote, "All stations
are so oriented that they serve others."

Fourth, the Bible teaches that, because of sin's devas-
tation, the high ideals of the work ethic can be attained
only through Christ's restoration, imparted to us in the
Gospel, and through the ministry of the Church.

The Fall has disrupted and obstructed the blessings
of work. Man cannot, and will not, work as he should
(Gen. 3:17–19). Sin blinds and binds us, so that our
divine commission is left unfulfilled. "Adam refused to
work as priest of God's creation," says theologian James
B. Jordan. "He rejected the true meaning and direction
of his life. As a result, he became dead and impotent, his
work was cursed to futility, and he was cast out of the
pleasant land of Eden into a howling wilderness."

As Langdon Lowe, a nineteenth-century Southern
Presbyterian, wrote, "Man was made for work. The Fall
unmade him. Now, in Christ made anew, man can once
again work. But he must be ever mindful of the salvific
connection: The call to work must not, cannot, go out
unaccompanied by the call to salvation."

In his groundbreaking book, *Idols for Destruction,*
Herbert Schlossberg states, "Christians ought not to support any policy toward the poor that does not seek to have
them occupy the same high plane of useful existence that
all of us are to exemplify. 'Serving the poor' is a euphe-
mism for destroying the poor unless it includes with it the
intention of seeing the poor begin to serve others."

Whereas humanitarian social policy keeps people help-
lessly dependent, Biblical charity seeks to remove them
from that status and return them to productive capacity.
Biblical charity seeks to put them back to work because
Biblical charity should never be anything other than a prod

to full restoration of the poor to their God-ordained calling. Paul makes it plain: "If a man will not work, he shall
not eat" (2 Thess. 3:10). Or, as Charles Haddon Spurgeon succinctly quipped, "He that gapes till he be fed,
will gape till he be dead. Nothing is to be got without
pains, except poverty and dirt." A handout does not charity make.

Every effort must be made to ensure that our helping
really does help. A handout may meet an immediate
need, but how does it contribute to the ultimate goal of
setting the recipient aright? How does it prepare him for
the job market? How does it equip him for the future?
How does it strengthen the family? How well does it
communicate the precepts of Biblical morality? The kind
of evangelical myopia that envisions the Scriptural duty
to the poor as a simple transfer of funds simply misses
the boat. When the Church mimics the government by
promiscuously dispensing groceries and other goods and
services, it hurts the poor more than it helps. Adherents
of such short-sighted thinking only perpetuate a "war
against the poor" rather than a "war on poverty." Authentic Christianity goes to work putting the able poor to
work. That's Biblical charity.

Sheaves for the Provident

In practice, how are these three elements—faith, family,
and work—coordinated into a coherent program of care
for the poor? Can these Biblical ideals be satisfactorily
implemented in a coherent and compassionate fashion?

Although contemporary examples abound, perhaps
the best illustration of Biblical charity in action is the
Scriptural narrative in the Book of Ruth. It is a story of
compelling beauty and romance, of faithfulness and in-

trigue, of tragedy and hope. Set during the time of the judges, it provides for us an intimate glimpse of covenant life in ancient Israel.

The main characters in the story, Ruth and Naomi, are widows living on the edge of destitution (Ruth 1:6–13). Determined to take responsibility for her elderly mother-in-law (Ruth 1:14) and to accept the terms of God's covenant for herself (Ruth 1:16–17), Ruth does the only thing she can do. She professes her faith, she preserves her family, and then she goes out to find work (Ruth 2:2). In many ways, though, this was a good news–bad news situation for her. The bad news was that Ruth was a stranger to the ways and customs of Israel, being a Moabitess (Ruth 1:4) and, furthermore, she did not appear to have any readily marketable skills. The good news was that God's Law made abundant and gracious provision for strangers (Ex. 23:9; Lev. 19:33–34; Dt. 24:17–18); as well as for unskilled, destitute workers (Lev. 19:9–10; 23:22; Dt. 23:24–25; 24:19–22). Gleaner laws stipulated that farmers and landowners leave the edges of their fields unharvested and that overlooked sheaves remain uncollected. Any among the poor or the alien who were willing to follow behind the harvesters and gather that grain were welcome to it, thereby "earning" their own keep. Ruth took advantage of just provision and was thus able to uphold her responsibility to Naomi.

Several basic principles concerning Biblical charity emerge from Ruth's story. *First,* it is clear that the full benefits of covenantal charity come into Ruth's purview only after she professed faith in the Lord. Whereas her sister-in-law, Orpah, turned away to the pagan gods of Moab—and thus to all their barrenness and privation— Ruth clung to Naomi, saying, "Don't urge me to leave you or to turn back from you. Where you go I will go, and where you stay I will stay. Your people will be my people and your God my God" (Ruth 1:16).

Ruth's whole way of thinking was transformed. Her vision of the future was corrected. Her hope was set on nothing less than the Lord of the covenant and His righteousness. This element of faith was essential in Ruth's rehabilitation from poverty to productivity. Biblical charity cannot successfully operate on any other basis.

Second, the apparatus for care that Ruth took advantage of was uniquely rooted in family life. Ruth didn't go out gleaning just anywhere. She went to the field of Boaz—having bonded herself to Naomi's family. She then invoked the Levirate code of redemption (Dt. 25:5–10).

Biblical charity relies on the principle of the kinsman redeemer as the first course of compassionate action. It attempts to rebuild and restore the natural bonds of the home and thus to provide a genuinely effectual safety net.

Third, Ruth worked. And she worked hard (Ruth 2:2–7). Gleaning the fields involved backbreaking labor. Biblical charity does not attempt to smooth over economic crisis by making privation somewhat more acceptable. It attempts to solve economic crisis. Biblical charity does not attempt to help families adjust to their situation. It attempts to change their situation. Biblical charity does not strive to make poverty and dependence more comfortable. It strives to make productivity and independence more attainable.

Notice that in all of this Ruth did not turn to the government for help in her time of distress. She looked to a decentralized private sector. Biblical charity is portrayed as a privately dispensed mercy ministry by the faithful, within the family, and through individual initiative, not by an overarching state institution (Ruth 2:4–16).

Welfare in the Bible is invariably private in nature. As a result, the apparatus of charity is kept simple. Accountability is enhanced. Flexibility is made possible. Local conditions are maximized. And personal attention is made more likely. By keeping charity deinstitutionalized, everyone concerned is saved from the anguish of graft, corruption, and red tape.

In our cosmopolitan culture of vast concentrations of urban poor, many have suggested that a faith-family-and-work-driven charitable structure is simply out of date. But as John Naisbitt has pointed out in his seminal work *Megatrends,* the "gleaning model" is as up-to-date as the latest high-tech Silicon Valley breakthrough: "Americans, especially senior citizens, are helping themselves by salvaging the vast food resources usually wasted in production and harvesting—about 20 percent of all food produced, according to the United States Agriculture Department. Gleaners' groups in Arizona, California, Michigan, Oregon, and Washington State go into the fields and find food passed over by the harvest, then distribute it in community groups. St. Mary's Food Bank in Phoenix, Arizona, which collects cast-aside and gleaned food, sent two million pounds of food to schools and social service groups and fed forty-eight thousand emergency victims for three days during 1979. Now St. Mary's helps other groups all across the country to learn the self-help approach to cutting waste and feeding the poor."

Other gleaners' groups, like Goodwill Industries, the Salvation Army, and Light and Life Resale Shops, collect discarded commodities and then repair them for sale by using unemployed and handicapped workers. And groups like HELP Services in Texas and the St. Vincent de Paul Society in New Hampshire have put unemployed workers out on the city streets cleaning up litter, rubbish, and overgrowth in exchange for groceries. All without federal subsidies. All without bureaucratic interference. R. J. Rushdoony has pointed out, "The rise of welfarism has limited the growth of urban gleaning, but its potentialities are very real and deserving greater development."

The "bootstrap" approach is fine as far as it goes, but we mustn't forget that Ruth did indeed obtain genuine mercy. She couldn't make it on her own. She needed help. And Boaz was compelled by a moral imperative to provide that help. But help was not a "right" that Ruth could claim or an entitlement that Boaz had to capitulate to.

Theodore Roosevelt once said, "There are those who believe that a new modernity demands a new morality. What they fail to consider is the harsh reality that there is no such thing as a new morality. There is only one morality. All else is immorality. There is only true Christian ethics over against which stands the whole of paganism. If we are to fulfill our great destiny as a people, then we must return to the old morality, the sole morality."

These three essential ingredients—faith, family, and work—enable charity to be rooted in that old morality, that sole morality and thus to accomplish the great aim of succoring the afflicted, protecting the innocent, and equipping the helpless.

6. NEW TESTAMENT DEVELOPMENTS: PRINCIPLES INTO ACTION

David W. Hall

A survey of New Testament principles by David Hall, including a more detailed treatment of 1 Timothy 5, yields revealed principles that can guide us in welfare reform today. The conclusion is a collage of convictions, showing the compatibility of this Biblical approach with the soundest of modern thought. With this study, a moratorium on leftist theology is declared, in anticipation of more balanced applications of Scripture to this and other societal issues. The day is long passed when the New Testament can be hijacked and pressed into service as handmaiden to a liberal agenda. Welfare reformed is the compassionate application of such New Testament teaching.

> *Although the Great Society and its many so-*
> *cial programs have had some good effects,*
> *there is a vast body of evidence suggesting*
> *that these "remedies" have reached the limits*
> *of their success. . . . Our social and civic*
> *institutions—families, churches, schools,*
> *neighborhoods, and civic classrooms—have*
> *traditionally taken on the responsibility of*
> *providing our children with love, order and*
> *discipline—of teaching self-control, compas-*
> *sion, tolerance, civility, honesty and respect*
> *for government. Government, even at its*
> *best, can never be more than an auxilary in*
> *the development of character. . . . The de-*
> *structive incentives of the welfare system are*
> *perhaps the most glaring examples of this.*[1]

While surveying the New Testament corpus on the subject of the poor and their treatment, one can quickly notice that most of these principles are entirely compatible with the previous Old Testament standards, reflecting, as might have been expected, a unity between the testaments. The New Testament, as well as the Old Testament, treats this subject, not assigning it the irrelevance some pietists might suggest.

However, from a less ideological review, and contrary to the predominant modern liberal perception of Jesus as a glorified "social worker *cum* political-activist-advocate for the oppressed" who constantly prattled about the poor and empowerment themes, relatively few teachings of Jesus normatively address the treatment of the economically poor. That may come as a surprise to many who have been taught otherwise, but a sober study of the matter will bear that out. In fact, only about ten separate and distinct teachings of Christ (surveyed below), out of the volume of His sayings, directly use the word "poor" in an economic sense. When this is recalled, it is perhaps more than anything a sign of the pervasive ideology of social liberalism, that the common image of Jesus as being nearly obsessed with the materially disadvantaged, is so widespread. It may be the case that Jesus has been conformed to the norms of the statist Great Society—recast as a Messianic welfare boss—and the corresponding Gospel accounts are read through this filter, rather than culture being judged by the standards of Christ. We definitely want to hear all that Jesus and the New Testament have for us on this subject, but at the same time, we will want to preserve our earlier hermeneutical principles, and not automatically interpret these teachings in light of our own society's welfare experimentation. If we allow Jesus to speak for Himself, we will pursue that kind of balance, and may also come up with some priorities different from some of the earlier evangelical theses which were represented as being undebatable.

First let it be noted, in agreement with the Old Testament norms, that there is a New Testament distinction between the poor in "spirit" and the poor in "economics." Mt. 5:3 makes this distinction overt from the outset of the Gospels, as Jesus qualifies the poor who receive this blessing, not as the generic poor, nor the poor apart from spiritual considerations, but specifically the "poor in spirit." The same phraseology in Luke 6:20 leads most to render this group as those who recognize, or humbly admit, their own spiritual inability and ineffectiveness.

This is not restricted to the materially disadvantaged, and even includes the materially wealthy who are Christians.

Still, in light of the above, the economically poor are distinguished and recognized as objects worthy of Christ's ministry. In Matthew 11:5 and Luke 7:22, Jesus singles out certain disadvantaged groups of the genuine needy—the blind, the lame, the leprous, the deaf—as the poor to whom the Gospel is preached. In Luke 4:18, Jesus announces, "The Spirit of the Lord is on me, because he has anointed me to preach good news to the poor," demonstrating that the poor are distinguishable, and not to be ignored as objects of the ministry. Later, in Luke 14:13, 21, in the setting of a parable, the poor are to be invited to a banquet hosted by those celebrating Christ's reign. So for Jesus, the poor are not invisible. He is not so ensconced in evangelical comfort or unconcerned as to eliminate the poor from the proper scope of the ministry of the church.

Indeed, the church is to care for the poor—just as in the Old Testament. Even in Jesus' own time, certain benevolent customs had been established to ameliorate this concern. Matthew 6:1–4 assumes the giving to the needy. The mandate to begin that kind of welfare is absent from this and other passages. Instead, it is *assumed* that true Christian piety will have among its components an emphasis on charitable and sacrificial giving to the poor. It was a given that the Jewish synagogue would be involved with remediation of the needs of the poor. Jesus taught, not as a higher principle but as a basic assumption, that His disciples would give to the poor in some helpful ways.

The point for our study is that Jesus neither altered nor originated the duty of believer to care for the poor.

The regulation in this passage is not concerned with the execution of this duty, only with the motivation and attitude with which it is performed. The giving to the needy is not to be animated by desire for recognition favoring the benefactors. The giving—again assumed in verse 3, "But when you give . . . "—is to be done as secretively as possible with true intent to help, not to bring glory to the giver. The reward from the Father in heaven is promised in verse 4. Behind this paragraph is the Jewish institution of almsgiving, which continued even into the times of the Reformation, when, for example, John Calvin, and others, chartered the office of Deacon to be involved in the distribution of alms. Such a church-based benevolent ministry is still widely used today, if called by other names, and some of the best welfare solutions are off-springs of this. It is not beyond the realm of the possible to have an even greater participation by churches in welfare in our own time.

Another facet of the New Testament teaching is that benevolent giving to the poor is sometimes an indicator of either obedience or greed. In addition to being a God-given duty, such Christian giving can also serve as a *de facto* readout of honest commitment to live as God prescribes. Jesus, on one occasion, says to a wealthy man as a test of his willingness to obey, "If you want to be perfect, go, sell your possessions and give to the poor, and you will have treasure in heaven" (Mt. 19:21, Mk. 10:21, Lk. 18:22). In this passage, the wealthy man valued his wealth more than obedience to Christ. The tenth commandment found him guilty, and he left a nondisciple. The willingness to give to the poor was a test, one failed by that man and many Christians today.

On another occasion, the result was opposite, even if the test was similar. Zaccheus, in repentance, did become a disciple of Jesus and gave one-half of his possessions to the poor (Lk. 19:8). The Pharisees failed this same test, as Jesus rebukes them for tithing (which should be done!) the minutiae of the law, yet they failed to give justice, mercy, and faithfulness (Mt. 23:23). Not giving to the poor revealed their true lack of spirituality. Often, whether or not one has compassion toward the poor is a sign of the genuineness of discipleship.

This should be balanced with the fact that the Gospels caution against a false or superficial compassion for the poor. In Matthew 26:9, some of the disciples become indignant over the extravagance of the anointing of Jesus before His death at Bethany. Viewing this as a waste, they remark, "This perfume could have been sold at a high price and the money given to the poor." Jesus rebukes them for this error, as He tells them they will always have the poor with them (Mt. 26:11), illustrating the Old Testament realism we've seen before. Jesus believed there was a place for bounty, and also that poverty would never be totally eradicated. In this case, the amount of one year's wages—as clarified by the parallel in Mark 14:5—was not too wasteful. The treatment of poverty is not absolutized and its amelioration cannot be the only variable in welfare reform. Jesus stresses, "The poor you will always have with you, and you can help them any time you want. But you will not always have me" (Mk. 14:7). This should balance our means and realistically expected ends. A little less utopianism, and a recognition that some motivation to help the poor stems from an absolutized remediation of poverty, or even envy at times, is in order.

Judas even models a false compassion for the poor, as he is expected to give to the poor (Jn. 13:29), but again from poor motive. Motives are important. A ministry to the poor, which takes itself with such severe Stylite asceticism, as to have no ongoing sense of the proper place for kingdom-joy and celebration, is a distortion of Scripture more aligned with radical movements of the sixteenth century and communitarian movements of the past two centuries, than with the Kingdom movement of Jesus in the first century. An imbalanced sense of compassion for the poor may be frequently recognized as another of the perennial emanations of gnosticism, or one of the many glumness-by-pietistic-hypersacrifices, exemplified in left-wing approaches to ministry to the poor.

Accordingly, another proposition can be deduced: Jesus taught the persistence (nonsolubility) of poverty. From the above (chiefly, the explicit Matthew 26:11 and Mark 14:7. Also see Deuteronomy 15:11.), we should factor into our norms that poverty, according to Jesus' magisterial saying, is not expected to be totally or effectively eliminated in this life. That it will always be a problem effects the levels of expectation and the goals of a welfare reform. For example, if one targets full employment, total health care, nationalized health insurance, and the abolition of incomes below a certain annual figure, that will substantially alter the welfare reform plans—if contrasted with an approach which stresses personal responsibility and familial productivity.

As one of the final utterances in our Lord's earthly ministry (Jn. 12:6), it is affirmed that Jesus was not insensitive to the poor. It was partially because Judas was a thief that Jesus responded as He did. Yet again, He reiterates, "Leave her alone. . . . You will always have the

poor among you, but you will not always have me"
(Jn. 12:7–8). Hence, adherence to Jesus and His teachings is even a higher priority than poverty relief, as an
absolutized goal. Jesus established neither relief shelters
nor Union missions. In terms of His activities, He
seemed convinced that poverty would continue as part of
the human condition, and He did not institute definite
vehicles to alleviate such. Such absence is a striking cor-
rective to the past century's portrayal of Christ. Our
Master Himself seemed reconciled to this continuing reality as an acceptable part of God's providence in this
age. Christians will remain loathe to rebel against His
stated understanding.

*Even the poor can give and should be encouraged to
tithe*. In Mark 12:42 and Luke 21:2–3, Jesus tells the parable about the poor widow who gave her mite. She gave
all she had, and is commended by these parables. Jesus
thereby encourages even the poor and widows to give
responsibly. None are exempted from tithing, and that
may be one important clue in reforming welfare. This is
one level of dignified participation which should not be
taken from the poor. It may even be a principle that,
while the poor are receiving, they should simultaneously
be taught to give, a lesson in divine economics that must
be included in successful welfare reform.

*Also, Jesus affirms that our material sustenance is
derived from providence*. In Matthew 6:25–34 He
teaches that the provender of life is given to birds, flowers, and by extension, to human beings by the providence
of God. Whatever our lot in life, be it relative wealth or
poverty, it is to be seen as flowing from the active providence of God in our lives. We are not to compare our
wealth with others, nor to worry about our apparent

lacks. Instead, believers rightly related to their Creator-Provider should trust Him and then act responsibly. When was the last time any welfare policy sought to ascertain, prior to giving aid, whether God's providence had bearing on a person's material poverty? Discernment, as Marvin Olasky suggests, was a part of welfare in a bygone day.[2]

Later, in the New Testament, Paul states in terms of this providence, "Now he who supplies seed to the sower and bread for food will also supply and increase your store of seed and will enlarge the harvest of your righteousness. You will be made rich in every way so that you can be generous on every occasion, and through us your generosity will result in thanksgiving to God" (2 Cor. 9:10–11). Providence, expressed materially, in many ways, is beyond human grasp or planning. A dependence on God's providence, without the shirking of personal responsibility, might be an important non-economic factor to be included in welfare reform. If it is recalled that the end targets of welfare reform will largely affect the programs of welfare, then these matters should be included as principles. Specifically, if poor people are taught that wealth is not guaranteed by the state, nor any other source and if wealth and health are not "rights" and if wealth is not the only factor for human dignity and if wealth is ultimately determined by the will of God, then perhaps the orientation toward personal responsibility will be less greed-motivated, and more practical.

Two other brief observations could be given. *One* is that Jesus was concerned with physical health, too. In a great many cases, healing was a partial remedy for welfare (cf. Mt. 12:11–12). Jesus did not seem oblivious to the connection between health and productivity. *Second,* He himself, on one occasion, assuredly issues the injunction to productivity. In the parable of the talents (Mt. 25:26–27), Jesus exhorts an individual to be productive and seek a return on his investment. Jesus did not disqualify such capital enhancement, but even encouraged productivity on assets. This could help welfare reform, as well as correct illegitimate caricatures of Jesus as inherently anti-capitalist.

Finally, in our Gospel survey, let it be noted that Jesus realized that the seat of social or personal problems was not based on the external environment, but came "out of the heart." In Matthew 15:19, Jesus taught that a whole list of societal ills, including, but not limited to, "murder, adultery, sexual immorality, theft, false testimony, slander" (note: these are defined in terms of the ten commandments, still in Jesus' time) originated—and thus should their cure be sought—in the human heart. If the individual is seen as responsible for the list of crimes, if these truly originate from the human heart, then any welfare reform which hopes to offset ill-effects stemming from these ought to aim more for change of heart, a largely non-economic and spiritual activity. Jesus recognized and identified the seat of this problem. Our efforts should not be contrary to His wisdom.

The institutional crown of New Testament compassion is seen in the regularization of this ministry by the officeholders who make up the diaconate. As part of obedience to the Law, and modeled upon the servanthood of our Master, the Church is to perpetually minister through deacons and other regular officers. A church without a diaconal focus is an incomplete church. C. E. B. Cranfield captures part of the genius of the church's diaconal calling: "It is the Church's enacted *amen* to its prayer of intercession for 'all those, who are any ways afflicted, or distressed, in mind, body, or estate,' the deed which seals the sincerity of our words, the activity which marches side by side with our praying as its indispensable companion."[3]

Continuing on to the final section of Biblical teaching, in the epistles, one can begin by noting that instruction about the poor is even less at the forefront of these portions. The materially poor are addressed in only 5–6 separate didactic portions of the New Testament epistles. For those suckled at the breast of liberal theological teaching about the poor in the latter half of the twentieth century, notation of this relative paucity of overt teaching on this area may be as much of a shock as it is a needed modification.

Another feature of New Testament welfare is that the saints' material needs were offset by other Christians. In many cases, the Christian church cared for its own, not abdicating that concern to the state. Paul takes a material gift from one group to another in Acts 21. In Romans 15:26, the Christians of Macedonia and Achaia have given a financial contribution to the saints in Jerusalem, to those unbeknownst to them personally, hundreds of miles away, in a time when travel and distances were much more difficult to conquer than our own day. Giving from one religious group to another is mentioned in 2 Corinthians 9:9 and 8:3. Thus, one aspect of the welfare of the New Testament is that like-minded churches helped their own. Galatians 6:10 is clear that Christians must first "do good to all people, especially to those who belong to the family of believers," indicating the necessity of the church caring for its own, rather than turning its own over to the state. One suspects that white evangelical churches in the U.S. may actually have more total recipients of state welfare among its own members than black churches, even though the percentages may be higher for black Americans. Still, the New Testament is clear that the church should care for their own before abdicating that high calling to others.

Consistent with what has gone before, according to the New Testament a ministry to the poor is not to be forgotten, even by the most spiritual. Paul, amidst theological controversy in Galatians 2:10, not only called for theological orthodoxy, but also prominently required that the poor not be forgotten. Churches should be reminded of this. And in all fairness, if we criticize the state for usurping part of the church's rightful jurisdiction, it must also be admitted that the church, in its period of pietistic retreat from liberalism, has also been guilty of abdicating this area. The state made a plausible case that the poor were not being cared for and moved in. Yet the modern church may be as guilty of surrender in this area as the state is of the totalitarian impulse. If the church is to advocate for welfare reform, she must also actively advocate and assume responsibility for caring for the materially disadvantaged.

Yet, as a balance, while giving to the poor is admirable, as 1 Corinthians 13:3 teaches, it is not absolutized, nor elevated to the level of *summa*. One can be very compassionate toward the poor, but if not loving in all its splendor and definition, then all the giving to the poor in the world, apart from proper attitudinal and heart concerns, is ill-conceived. Even if we give our bodies over to asceticism, or give all our goods to the poor, if we do so without love for God and others, and if we carry about the attitude of pride in suffering or are animated by envy or assorted yearnings for equal redistributionism without love we are nothing.

Furthermore, Christians can rejoice even in environments of material poverty. Paul gives us many examples, and in 2 Corinthians 6:10, he urges others to do the same. The perspective of poverty can, at times, help us to understand others better, cause us to return to thankfulness to God who "giveth and taketh away," and redefine priorities with clarity.

Of course, in the New Testament, favoritism, particularly to discriminate against the poor *qua* poor is not to be sanctioned (see Jas. 2:2–7), and the rich who do oppress are roundly condemned (Jas. 5:1–6). Paul warns Timothy against the "love of money as the root of all evil" (1 Tim. 6:10) and counsels "godliness with contentment as great gain" (1 Tim. 6:6). It hardly needs reiterating that the New Testament is as strongly opposed as possible to covetousness, greed, theft, or any dependence on wealth or riches. And as already referenced, James 1:27 defines two clear groups in genuine need of assistance, the widows and orphans.

All in all, likely one of the best rounded portions of New Testament teaching on welfare models is found in 1 Timothy 5: 3–16. In that passage, the church is given the priority of responsibility in ministering to one genuinely needy segment, widows. If that segment of ministry were taken as embodying principles applicable to other welfare recipients, we might be in better shape.

According to this passage, first a determination is to be made if widows are really in need (v. 3). That very qualification implies the ancient distinction between the deserving poor and the undeserving, or between the truly needy as opposed to those who are capable of other sources of help. Even after that determination is made, once it is agreed that a widow is truly needy, and not in a condition of need due to her own fault or irresponsibility, the church does not move in to supplement immediately. Another agency of responsible welfare stands between the truly disadvantaged and the church.

Prior to the church helping, even if motivated by generosity, the next verse stipulates that if such a truly needy widow has children, or grandchildren (the family), "these should learn first of all to put their religion into practice by caring for their own family and so repaying their parents and grandparents, for this is pleasing to God" (1 Tim. 5:4). So first, personal responsibility is determined, followed by extended family aid. The "widow who is really in need" (1 Tim. 5:5) is in a tenuous situation and deserves special care. Nevertheless, as long as there are family members who can assume her care, they should do so first. The intensity of God's commitment to these steps of responsibility is evidenced by the strong saying in v. 8: "If anyone does not provide for his relatives, and especially for his immediate family, he has denied the faith and is worse than an unbeliever." Notice that there is no explicit distinction in this requirement between Christian or non-Christian. So immutable is God's mandate in this area, that one may actually declare by his outward actions that inwardly he is an unbeliever if he abdicates in caring for the truly needy in his own family.

Later, in 1 Timothy 5:16, we see another example: "If any woman who is a believer has widows in her family, she should help them and not let the church be burdened with them, so that the church can help those widows who are really in need." Again, the church is not the first resort, nor is the government. First, the person is responsible to work. Secondly, if they cannot provide for themselves—and it is genuine need—the family is to provide. Only then, if between those two industrious agencies the persons cannot make it, does the church step in. To step in prematurely—before those two sectors are given the challenge and the chance to dispense welfare—is to rob others of Christian ministry (even if they wish to be so pilfered), to violate God's prescribed order, and to encourage attitudes of dependency, forbidden by God's Word. Neither the church nor the state is licensed to assist prior to these agencies of responsibility.

This passage also teaches that aid to the truly needy may be linked to moral lifestyles, as well as the requirement for the recipient to help in constructive ministry. There is both an age qualification (1 Tim. 5:9), as well as a moral requirement of sexual faithfulness in this welfare plan. (Both AIDS and welfare reform could be helped by the integrity of some such proviso.) It does not appear that God considers it wrong, unduly burdensome, nor an imposition of values, to require moral and work-ethic stipulations to welfare recipients. Furthermore, the widow who receives from the church is to be known to the church (not a passerby looking for $25 for the electric bill), "for her good deeds, such as bringing up her children [there's family again], showing hospitality, washing the feet of the saints, helping those in trouble and devoting herself to all kinds of good deeds" (1 Tim. 5:10). This is not the slovenly person who sits idly by awaiting a monthly dole payment.

Further material assistance is prohibited to those who are idle (vv. 13–14), gossips (v. 13), busybodies (v. 13), or lustful after men (v. 11). This portion of Scripture positively sanctions the tying of material aid to godly lifestyles. Is that principle so mendicant, as not to merit reintroduction to a pitifully failed system?

And the proposed remedy for those unstable and younger widows is none other than the counsel to be reinjected into a family. Paul states by the inspiration of the Holy Spirit, "So I counsel younger widows to marry, to have children, to manage [a word from which economics is derived] their homes and to give the enemy no opportunity for slander" (1 Tim. 5:14). Thus, an order of responsibility is given, a full-orbed welfare structure with personal work ethic, family responsibility, and moral requirements. Perhaps the most amazing thing is that this was given two thousand years ago, and still provides the most promising values at the forefront of welfare reform in our own time.

In sum, the New Testament (as well as the Old Testament) gives us definite patterns for ministry to the poor and successful structures for welfare. Perhaps this passage is the single best pattern, where the following principles are exhibited. Any attempt at welfare reform would be foolish (or supremely arrogant) to ignore such a tried-and-proven institution, especially when it is noted that the origin of this pattern is not some task force, government commission, or imitation of a socialist flop; rather originated from the omniscient One who created persons, society itself, and who knows which combinations work best.

Finally, it should be noted that, in addition to giving protology, the Bible also proffers an eschatology. Revelation 21–22 describes the eventual elimination of poverty and the need for attendant welfare. Just as Jesus promised that "The poor you will always have with you" on this earth, there is also a time coming in which the poor will be no more. In this heavenly Jerusalem, typified by gold, silver, and precious stones, there will be no murders nor liars (Rev. 21:8). Society will need no entitlements, depending on God directly for light, glory, and honor (Rev. 21:23–26). Moreover, its inhabitants will have none of the sinful traits associated with sinful life-styles (Rev. 21:27). There will be an abundance of pure water (22:1), wealth (21:9–21), crops (22:2), vegetation (22:2), international healing and peace (22:2), as well as the absence of darkness (22:5). However, the Christian faith is careful to identify that truly utopian society only with the era of the millennium.

Conclusions

The New Testament and the Old Testament exhibit the same broad themes, a token of the unity between these testaments, attributable to common divine authorship (2 Tim. 3:16). It is also clarified that there will be a persistent tension between the "now" and the "not yet." The Christian caught between worlds is, therefore, to act responsibly to the "now" commands and duties of Scripture, but limit his expectations in light of the "not yet" character of the universe. A little less utopianism is greatly needed. The poor must remain subjects of concern for the church, but perhaps not preferentially so; rather in a balanced perspective. It is hoped that if providence and responsibility, justice and charity, can be held in tandem, that welfare reform to help the poor will neither be forgotten, nor elevated to the *summa*. These guiding principles cannot conceivably do worse in the long run than the previous experiments. Indeed, they hold promise of success, based on divine wisdom and proven efficacy.

Synthetically, the following propositions may be put together now about this subject.

1. There is a Scriptural distinction between the material poor and the spiritual poor. In application, this distinction needs to be kept clear, lest confusion of the categories lead to error.

2. The bulk of Scripture addresses remedy to spiritual poverty; yet material poverty is recognized, and in proper order, should be attended to by individual Christians and churches.

3. Material poverty has various causes, and correspondingly, various remedies.

4. The proper remedy stems from the cause. Again, distinctions are needed. It will hardly promise efficacy to seek to issue one kind of welfare for all sorts of problems. Discernment is greatly needed. One will continue to frustrate true compassion if money is doled out when root moral issues are more deserving of attention. Likewise, the dispensing of moral exhortation alone misses the mark if there is true material need (cf. Mt. 25).

5. Some of the causes of material poverty are:

   a. *Sloth.* As George Grant summarizes: "The teaching on sluggards is clear and precise. The Bible says that sluggards waste opportunities (Prov. 10:4), are victims of self-inflicted bondage (Prov. 12:24), and are unable to accomplish anything in life (Prov. 15:19). A sluggard is boastful (Prov. 10:26), lustful (Prov. 13:4), wasteful (Prov. 12:27), improvident (Prov. 20:4), and lazy (Prov. 24:30–34). He is self-deceived (Prov. 26:16), neglectful (Eccl. 10:18), unproductive (Mt. 25:26), and impatient (Heb. 6:12)."[4]

   b. *Providence.* Another cause of poverty is the outworking of God's decree in our lives. This may extend to two possible horizons:

      1. *General,* as our "lot in life", or

2. *Episodic,* due to tragedy, natural disaster, chastening, or even for times of specific instruction by God.

c. *Poor planning, or lack of saving for emergency* (as in Proverbs).

d. *God's curse on a land.*

e. *Sinful choices or lifestyles.*

f. *Injustice* (Is. 58 and Amos above) or exploitation of the poor (Jas. 5:1–2 and Amos 4).

6. If the cause is rooted in providence, then we must accept that as being from God. However, if the cause of poverty is rooted in human responsibility (or slothfulness), then we may seek to change. Even the left-leaning U.S. Catholic Bishops Letter (1984–5) advocated that "public-assistance programs should encourage rather than penalize gainful employment."[5] Improvement of one's estate or wealth is not sinful in itself; only if actuated by greed. Otherwise, the Scriptural assumption is that one will be encouraged to own property, develop it, and enhance it so that he can support the family, tithe, contribute to other charities, and leave an inheritance for children. Once the question of providence is determined, the person is free to work their way out of their impoverishment.

7. Roles for alleviation of poverty depend on a prioritized order, from (1) personal industriousness to (2) family to (3) church, as 1 Timothy 5 displays most clearly. Again, a New Testament warrant for the state doling out welfare is absent. One can certainly argue from silence on this, but it

should be admitted that at best, it is an argument from silence, despite the New Testament's nonsilence in chartering the state to perform certain functions in Romans 12. Still, it must be maintained, to be Christian at all, that the State should only be involved in cases of last resort (as in Thielicke's "minimalist state"). That is to say, the state should supply assistance *only* if (1) there are cases of moral lifestyle, where obedience to God's ways are kept with willingness to work. Thereafter, the state *at most* could be warranted— and this only by inference—to assist those (2) who are working, (3) who are truly disabled in some way, (4) who have no family, either generations above or below who can be called on to assist, or (5) who have no church to assume penultimate responsibility. Prior to the state giving aid, these five requirements must be exhausted.

To my friends who categorically say there is no room for state welfare at all, call me pragmatic, but I'd be willing to allow the state to aid any who pass the above means test, including the prerequisite that they join a functioning local church, prior to assistance (on the analogy of 1 Tim. 5:10). I feel safe in asserting that such a state-based welfare could not, if adhered to, possibly mutate into the kind of system we presently have. If those criteria were met, the welfare budget *for adults* would immediately be shrunk by 90 percent because those who have illegitimate births, AIDS due to immoral behavior, poverty without at least some work, unbelievers who refuse to participate in a church of their choice, and many other adults would be disqualified. That would leave the chief needs to widows—male and female in aged conditions—and orphans, right back to the earlier study commissioned about A.D. 50, as reported in James 1:27.

8. In addition, at some point, the caveat must be issued that there is no realistic way around the consequent inequities in relative wealth which result when viewed from this perspective of providence and responsibility (Ex. 23). The death of egalitarianism, in its seemingly infinite forms, must follow from the acceptance of these Biblical norms.

Biblically we must overcome the paranoia of asserting that personal responsibility is to be taught. Just what a reformed welfare model would look like if incorporating the above norms, may not be certain. This study certainly does not profess to suggest a specific model, much less an all-encompassing programmatic solution. It has sought to elucidate Biblical norms and principles. They may be summarized below, in short form (with the Affirmations and Denials in this volume as a fuller form of expression). It is hoped that if wisely incorporated they would yield benefit to the poor, and righteousness in society.

- Supportive of fruitfulness and productivity
- Will encourage private ownership and development of property
- Looks to the family, first of all, for alleviation and assistance
- Based on the constitution of the Ten Commandments
- Situations aren't brand new
- Respects the principle of restitution
- Paternal responsibility upheld

- Equity (nonpreferentiality) of justice to the poor and nonpoor
- Fairness in paying wages and levying assessments
- Principle of responsibility, not necessarily absolute equality
- Encourages honest labor; not handouts
- Observes the distinction between causes of poverty
- Obligation to care for poor
- Blessing to those who care for the poor.

Warren Brookes is quoted as writing, "nothing can begin to match the systematic degradation, dehumanization, and cultural genocide that has been wreaked on black Americans"[6] by the welfare state. If Christians are to see welfare reform, that is reform according to Biblical principles, they would do well to remember the suggested characteristics recommended by James Gwartney and Thomas McCaleb, who prescribe the following:

- Any welfare reform should be "altered so as to reinforce and not subvert such traditional norms as work, intact families, and childbearing within marriage," recognizing the legitimacy of "family, church, private charity, and community action in the alleviation of poverty."
- The welfare system "should be reformed so as to give proper recognition to the importance" of voluntary organizations, churches, and those structures which "reinforce certain traditional values that encourage individual, parental, and family responsibility."
- Welfare "recipients should not be allowed to use children as hostages in order to blackmail society." Ways should be sought to alter the incentives that encourage such activity.

- New approaches to workfare, to encourage personal responsibility and the integrity of child support legislation, should be promoted.[7]

Too often we have been unwilling to face up to the role of financial incentive, believing that the anthropology of modernism had exceeded such erstwhile confines. Long ago, it was recognized that financial incentive helped encourage industriousness. In a prototype of what would come to be known as the protestant work ethic expressed in capitalism, John Knox (in 1560) said of ministers and their need for compensation (but the point has broader application), "It is not to be supposed that each man will dedicate himself . . . to serve his church, that they look for no worldly commodity. But this cankered nature which we bear is provoked to follow virtue when it sees honor and profit annexed to the same."[8]

A renewal of the proper role for monetary incentive would also be helpful for welfare reform. Further, it might be worthwhile to review other aspects of ancient wisdom, as John Knox and other reformation leaders sound quite reminiscent of Saint Paul in 1 Timothy 5, prioritizing first industry and personal responsibility, then family, and finally the church. This structured responsibility also reflects the same views of anthropology that late-twentieth century welfare reform is being forced to recognize.

As to the centrality of the church in welfare alleviation, George Grant comments: "In fact, so central was welfare to the task of the disciples that even the structure of the Church was custom-designed to facilitate its efficient execution."[9] He also cites,

A U.S. Senate subcommittee report estimated that if every Christian family would only take care of its own, the federal dole would decrease a full 30 percent. If every Church would then take care of *its* own, the dole would decrease another 12 percent. And then, if each of those Churches would provide a sponsoring family to exercise charity to a single outsider, the federal dole could be eliminated completely.

"Let the Church be the Church" might well be one of the rallying cries for true welfare reform. Perhaps the regulators can overlook the imagined "wall of separation" liberating the church to once again do her job.[10]

If the church is to be the church, she must redouble her efforts at caring for the poor in modes which do not share the statist foundation. The state could even delegate welfare to proven private agencies which have existing programs to support the values stated above. The federal government could commit itself, in principle, to phasing itself out of the welfare business over a twenty-year period, with funding for the next twenty years being divided among the states on a per capita basis. Each state could then seek to delegate the care for the poor to responsible private groups that (and *only that*) maintain the above values. To those groups subsidies should be paid in lieu of the state caring for the poor. In time, even the individual states would phase themselves out of the welfare business, with private, value-based groups doing a better and more personal job, spending less overall, costing the taxpayers considerably less, and finally weaning expectations for welfare away from statist agencies.

Certainly this proposal has difficulties, but hardly more than the existing system. If one is pining for a problemless approach, no welfare reform, nor assistances will ever develop. This Biblical approach also holds great promise. It could actually help.

Frederick Herzog trenchantly observes what happens when the church, in her diaconal ministry to the poor, really takes her charge seriously. He records,

> When during World War II the Netherlands were occupied by Germany the deacons of the Dutch Reformed Church assumed the care for the politically persecuted, supplying food and providing secret refuge. Realizing what was happening, the Germans decreed that the elective office of the deacon should be eliminated. The Reformed Synod on 17 July 1941 resolved: "Whoever touches the diaconate interferes with what Christ has ordained as the task of the Church. He touches the cult of the Church." Whoever lays hands on diakonia lays hands on worship! The Germans backed down. In taking diakonia seriously in a concrete political situation the Church begins to grasp her very being.[11]

7. POVERTY: A PROBLEM IN NEED OF DEFINITION

E. Calvin Beisner

Cal Beisner, author and lecturer at Covenant College offers a rarity—an empirical study of the first order by an evangelical thinker, with several sturdy arguments against a relative definition of poverty. Only when we place a Biblical definition on poverty can we sort out some of the inflated claims swirling about us. An excellent study like this one, with a healthy perspective seldom heard—even among evangelicals—is essential to form a foundation for welfare that truly cares for the poor.

> *Subsidizing sluggards is the same as subsidizing evil. It is subsidizing dependence. It is ultimately subsidizing slavery—moral slavery, and then physical slavery. On the other hand, refusing to care for the oppressed is the same as endorsing evil. It is endorsing injustice. It is ultimately endorsing slavery—again, moral and physical[1] ... It is not those who say, "The poor! The poor!" who will enter the Kingdom of Heaven, but those who actually put in place an economic system that helps the poor no longer to be poor.[2]*

*I*n January, 1990, Dr. Joe Remenyi, an Australian economist, presented to the Oxford Conference on Christian Faith and Economics a fine paper titled "Income Generation By the Poor: A Study of Credit-based Income and Employment Generation Programs in Developing Countries," since published as a short book titled *Where Credit Is Due*.[3] I heartily recommend it to anyone interested in learning what kinds of development really work in less-developed countries.

The major task of Dr. Remenyi's paper was to review about a dozen programs located in less-developed countries of Asia, Africa, and Latin America whose purpose was to put into the hands of low-income people capital loans that they could use to start or expand micro-enterprises. Dr. Remenyi's conclusion was that such programs were far more effective at helping people raise their incomes than were direct handouts and other more traditional development programs because they enabled people to become wealth creators themselves, tied them directly into the sowing-and-reaping process, and helped them to exercise responsibility. He also found that the poor recipients of these loans, most of which bore interest, had significantly higher rates of repayment than did most borrowers in the conventional loan market, despite their having had little or no credit record and little or no collateral before participating in the programs.

While I applauded Dr. Remenyi's study, my applause, however, came with a reservation. Because the paper focused on income generation by the *poor,* and on credit-providing programs aimed to facilitate income generation by the *poor,* it was necessary at the outset that Dr. Remenyi state what he meant by *the poor.* This is what he said:

> To be poor, in the economic sense, one merely has to have a sufficiently low income relative to the national average. In this study the standard below which one is regarded as poor is defined as an annual income less than one half of the national [gross domestic product] per head. On this basis it is evident that to be poor is the norm in most developing countries. This fact is critical if we are to target development to benefit the poor. If one further defines the poor as those who belong to households with an annual income of half the national GDP per capita or less, we define as poor between one half and three quarters of the households of developing countries. In other words, the poor are where the bulk of the people are.[4]

Dr. Remenyi's working definition of the poor was in every respect consistent with the common definition used by economists worldwide. It has, however, no rational basis, and much sensible criticism may be leveled against it. Consider four points.

The Relative Definition Is Arbitrary

First, the relative definition of poverty is simply arbitrary. Why pick 50 percent of a nation's GNP or GDP per capita as the poverty threshold? Why not 45 percent, or 55 percent, or 60 percent, or 40 percent? Wherever we draw the line, so long as we draw it only on the basis of choosing a percentage of average income, we will have no reasonable grounds for not drawing it a point or two lower or a point or two higher. Furthermore, why make a *nation's* gross product per capita the measuring stick? Why not a *continent's?* Why not a *city's,* or a *state's,* or the *world's?* This last option would have more appeal for Christians, who are taught in the Parable of the Good Samaritan that national lines do not define who one's neighbors are.

The Relative Definition Is Self-Contradictory

Second, the relative definition leads to self-contradiction. If national product per capita is the standard of comparison rather than world product per capita, the irrational conclusion arises that some people with more wealth are poorer than others with less.

Dr. Remenyi printed a table as part of his paper showing income distribution and gross national product per capita in selected countries, by which he sought to demonstrate the huge proportions of various populations that were poor. The table divided the countries into three geographical groups—Asia, Africa, and Latin America—plus one group of donor countries, nations that contribute material aid to the poor of other countries. Within each group, the nations were listed in order of ascending GNP per capita. As I read the table, several questions presented themselves: Granted the relative definition of poverty, what would be the poverty levels in these different nations? And what would be the result of comparing increasingly severe levels of relative poverty across nations? Here—taking the countries Dr. Remenyi listed, and using the GNP per capita data he supplied—is a summary of what I found. (See Table 1.)

Consider Asia. In Hong Kong, one was poor if his income fell below $3,115 per year. In South Korea, however, one was not poor unless his annual income fell below $1,075—meaning that a citizen of Hong Kong could make nearly three times as much as a citizen of Korea, and the Korean would not be poor but the person in Hong Kong would be. In Malaysia, the poverty threshold was $1,000 per year; in Thailand, a mere $400; in the Philippines, $290; in Indonesia, $265; in Sri Lanka, $190; in India, $135; and in Bangladesh, $75. Incredibly, a citizen of Hong Kong making forty-one times as much as a citizen of Bangladesh could be called poor while the Bangladeshi was not called poor.

Look now to Africa. A Mauritian was poor if his annual income fell short of $545, but a person in the Ivory Coast could make as little as $331 and not be poor. The threshold in Egypt was $305; in Zambia, $195; and in Kenya, $145. The spread in Africa was not so wide, then, as that in Asia, but it was significant nonetheless. A Kenyan, to be disqualified for poverty relief, could make as little as $145 per year, while a Mauritian could make 3.75 times as much and still qualify.

And now Latin America. There the spread was about the same as in Africa, although the base numbers were nearly three times as high. A Venezuelan was poor if he made less than $1,540; an Argentinean, if he made less than $1,065; a Panamanian, less than $1,050; a Mexican, less than $1,040; a Brazilian, less than $820; a Pe-

ruvian, less than $505; and a Salvadoran, less than $410.
The Salvadoran, then, could not qualify as poor unless
his income was less than one-third that of a poor Venezuelan's.

Table 1 Comparative Poverty Incomes Based on Relative Definitions of Poverty					
Group/ Country	GNP/ Capita (1985 US$)	Poverty Threshold (at 50% of GNP/cap.)	Severity of Poverty as Percent of GNP/cap. (increasing as percent of GNP/cap. received falls)	Annual Income Received at Severity Level (1985 US$)	Income Up (+) or Down (-) with Increasing Severity of Poverty
Asia					
Bangladesh	150	75.00	49	73.50	n.a.
India	270	135.00	44	121.50	+
Sri Lanka	380	190.00	39	148.20	+
Indonesia	530	265.00	34	180.20	+
Philippines	580	290.00	29	168.20	+
Thailand	800	400.00	24	192.00	+
Malaysia	2,000	1,000.00	19	380.00	+
S. Korea	2,150	1,075.00	14	301.00	-
Hong Kong	6,230	3,115.00	9	560.70	+
Simple Aveage	**1,455**	**727.50**	**29**	**421.95**	**n.a.**
Africa					
Kenya	290	145.00	49	142.10	n.a.
Zambia	390	195.00	44	171.60	+

Group/ Country	GNP/ Capita (1985 US$)	Poverty Threshold (at 50% of GNP/cap.)	Severity of Poverty as Percent of GNP/cap. (increasing as percent of GNP/cap. received falls)	Annual Income Received at Severity Level (1985 US$)	Income Up (+) or Down (-) with Increasing Severity of Poverty
Egypt	610	305.00	39	237.90	+
Ivory Coast	660	330.00	34	224.40	-
Mauritius	1,090	545.00	29	316.10	+
Simple Average	*610*	*305.00*	*39*	*237.90*	*n.a.*
Latin America					
El Salvador	820	410.00	49	401.80	n.a.
Peru	1,010	505.00	44	444.40	+
Brazil	1,640	820.00	39	639.60	+
Mexico	2,080	1,040.00	34	707.20	+
Panama	2,100	1,050.00	29	609.00	-
Argentina	2,130	1,065.00	24	511.20	-
Venezuela	3,080	1,540.00	19	585.20	+
Simple Average	*1,840*	*920.00*	*34*	*625.60*	*n.a.*
Donors					
Britain	8,870	4,435.00	49	4,346.30	n.a.
Netherlands	10,020	5,010.00	44	4,408.80	+
Australia	11,920	5,960.00	39	4,648.80	+
W. Germany	12,080	6,040.00	34	4,107.20	-
Japan	12,840	6,420.00	29	3,723.60	-
Canada	14,120	7,060.00	24	3,388.80	-

Group/ Country	GNP/ Capita (1985 US$)	Poverty Threshold (at 50% of GNP/cap.)	Severity of Poverty as Percent of GNP/cap. (increasing as percent of GNP/cap. received falls)	Annual Income Received at Severity Level (1985 US$)	Income Up (+) or Down (-) with Increasing Severity of Poverty
Norway	15,400	7,700.00	19	2,926.00	-
United States	17,480	8,740.00	14	2,447.20	-
Simple Average	*12,840*	*6,420.00*	*31.5*	*4,044.60*	*n.a.*

I need hardly belabor how absurd the relative poverty levels can become when we compare the poor in donor nations of the developed world with the poor—or even the middle class—in any of the nations of the less-developed world. Suffice it to say that an American was poor if his income fell below $8,740; a Bangladeshi was not poor unless his income was less than 1/116th as much. Clearly there is something wrong with our definition of poverty when one can be called poor in one country with an income more than four times as high as the average income, and more than eight times as high as the poverty threshold, in South Korea.

Absurd as these observations make the relative definition of poverty appear, they do not push the definition to its extreme. Consider what happens if we look not just at poverty thresholds but at increasingly severe levels of poverty. Let me explain. If the poverty threshold is defined as income below 50 percent of gross national (or domestic) product per capita, then it follows that someone with an income of 44 percent of GNP per capita should be poorer than someone with 49 percent; that someone with 39 percent should be poorer yet; someone with 34 percent still poorer; and so on. Within a given country, that of course is true. An Egyptian earning 49 percent of GNP per capita has income of $299, while one earning 44 percent has income of $268, and one earning 39 percent has income of only $238.

But a strange thing happens if we compare someone in more severe poverty in India with someone in less severe poverty in Bangladesh. The Indian earning 44 percent of GNP per capita has income of $122, while the Bangladeshi earning 49 percent has income of only $73.50. So the poorer Indian is richer than the richer Bangladeshi. Should you wonder whether such things can really be so, let me assure you, they can. The still poorer Sri Lankan, at 39 percent of GNP per capita, can be earning more than twice as much as his richer Bangladeshi neighbor. And the yet poorer Indonesian, at 34 percent of GNP per capita, can be earning nearly two-and-a-half times as much as his richer Bangladeshi neighbor. And the piteously poor citizen of Hong Kong, earning only 9 percent of GNP per capita, can have income over seven-and-a-half times as high as his richer Bangladeshi neighbor. Meanwhile, the desperately poor American, earning 14 percent of GNP per capita, has income more than 33 times as high as his richer Bangladeshi neighbor. (For complete comparisons, see Table 1.)

Any definition of poverty that leads inexorably to such absurdities is itself absurd.

The Relative Definition
Makes Eliminating Poverty Impossible

Third, the relative definition of poverty makes the elimination of poverty, and even its reduction in incidence, nearly impossible. It follows necessarily from a relative notion of poverty that unless all people in a society have precisely equal shares of wealth (or income, if that is the focus of concern), it must be impossible to eradicate poverty or even greatly to reduce its prevalence in society, no matter how much wealth (or how high an income) even the least wealthy members of the society enjoy. In anything but a successfully communist society (which has never existed), there will always be differences in income based on circumstance, personal choices, abilities, and a variety of other factors.

Policy analyst Robert Rector makes this point clear:

> Material poverty means, in the simplest sense, having a family income below the official poverty income threshold, which was $12,675 for a family of four in 1991. To the average American, however, to say someone is poor implies that he or she is malnourished, inadequately clothed, and lives in inadequate housing. There is little material poverty in the United States in this sense. . . . Today, the fifth of the population with the lowest incomes has a level of economic consumption higher than that of the median American family in 1955. . . . People defined by the U.S. government as "poor" have almost the same average level of consumption of protein, vitamins, and other nutrients as people in the upper middle class. . . . The principal nutrition-related problem facing poor people in the United States today is obesity, not hunger. . . . [A] "poor" American has more housing space and is less likely to be overcrowded than is the *average* citizen in *Western* (second italics added) Europe. . . . [N]early 40 percent of the households defined as poor by the government own their own homes.[5]

There will always be those with more than the average income, those with the average income, and those with less than the average income. And if history is our teacher, it appears that there will always be those with less than half the average income. In the United States, for instance, "the percentage of income that is received by each quintile group is very close to that received by the same quintile group in 1776. According to those statistics, we have made no improvement in the *position* of the poor over the last 200 years. But is that relevant? One must not ignore the fact that those people at the bottom have substantially improved their ability to consume food, enjoy medical care and have more of other economic goods."[6] What sense does it make to call poor today Americans whose standard of living is several times higher than that of the *top* 20 percent of Americans a century ago?

Relative Definitions of Poverty Rely on Unreliable Data

Fourth, calculations of poverty rates based on a relative definition rely on unreliable national population, income, and distribution statistics that bias results toward greater incidence of poverty. Reliance on statistical reporting of GNP and GNP per capita for one's definition of poverty and for the practical application of that definition within given economies is tenuous at best and notoriously misleading at worst—which is the most likely case in the less-developed economies, where "the biases and errors of income estimates . . . often amount to several hundred per cent"[7] and statistics on the distribution of income are even less reliable than statistics on GNP and GNP per capita.[8] Examples of flaws in GNP per capita (and GNP) estimates that are particularly pervasive in studies of less-developed countries include:

1. Failure to quantify and include the value of home production of food and clothing in poorer house-

holds, a value that often is very high relative to that of cash income earned on the job, frequently exceeding cash income by several times over. (The result is to greatly exaggerate the apparent number of the poor.);

2. Failure, in international comparisons, to deal adequately with purchasing power parities, which, for example, make earnings in India able to purchase about three times as much there as equivalent earnings (at official exchange rates) would purchase in the United States. (The result is to exaggerate both the severity and the rates of poverty in some countries and to underestimate them in others.);

3. Failure to consider differences in age distribution from one country to another. (Age distribution heavily affects economic production and consumption needs. Children typically need far less income than adults.);

4. Often large inaccuracies in population estimates—in less-developed countries usually on the high side—that skew product per capita figures sharply downward.

Consider that last point a little more closely. International organizations dedicated to slowing or reversing world population growth have demonstrated a strong tendency to overestimate population in less-developed countries. I will not speculate here on their motives for doing so, but the tendency is demonstrable, and it results in significant underestimates of gross product per capita.

Such are the *Alice in Wonderland* problems of a relative definition of poverty. Up becomes down, richer becomes poorer, and poorer becomes richer. And the effect of all this on people who care and want to take sensible steps to help is to confuse them and divert their attention—and their gifts—from the needier to the less needy. "Woe," said Isaiah, "to those who call evil good and good evil, who put darkness for light and light for darkness, who put bitter for sweet and sweet for bitter" (Is. 5:20). Yes, and woe to those who put rich for poor and poor for rich!

For people called upon to be neighbors to people in need across national lines, defining poverty on a nation-specific, relative basis should be simply unacceptable. When it results in our pouring billions of dollars into "poverty relief" to Americans, making that assistance unavailable to our truly poor neighbors in the less-developed world who are literally a hundred times worse off than the recipients of our generosity here, it is simply scandalous.

The Need for a Biblical Definition of Poverty

The absurdities implied by relative definitions of poverty fairly cry out to be alleviated by adopting an absolute definition. And, indeed, until recently such a definition was commonly used and is still reflected in standard dictionaries. Thus, an authoritative modern dictionary defines *poor* as describing one who is "lacking material possessions; having little or no means to support oneself; needy," and *poverty* as "indigence, lack of means of *subsistence*."[9] A modern encyclopedia defines poverty as "an insufficiency of the material *necessities of life*."[10] And an older dictionary defines poverty as "need or scarcity of means of subsistence; needy circumstances; indigence; penury."[11] These definitions are all absolute and all have to do with the means of subsistence, i.e., "the material necessities of life."

Interestingly enough, an exhaustive study of the Biblical vocabulary of poverty and its usage shows that this is precisely what the Bible means by *poverty,* when it speaks of material poverty.[12] In the New Testament, for instance, we find reference to three economic classes:

1. The first group is the rich, for whom the word is *ploúsios,* need not work to survive, or even to thrive, but can live entirely on the earnings of their investments in others' labor. (This does not mean that the Bible assumes that the rich never work. They may work, and many work very hard.)

2. The second group consists of those who lack none of their daily necessities, but who do not have sufficient wealth to hire others to do their work for them. These people, the *pénes,* may be identified with those today who must work for a living rather than living on the interest and dividends of savings and investments. It is common to translate *pénes* "poor." If this is understood simply to mean "not rich," it may be unobjectionable. But if it implies destitution or need for charitable support, it is certainly wrong. The noun comes from the verb *pénamai,* "to work for one's living." As such it might better be translated, in its only occurrence in the New Testament (2 Cor. 9:9), "laborer."[13]

3. The third group consists of people who are so destitute that they must depend on charity for survival. They cannot sustain themselves, usually because they are too old or young or handicapped

to work. These, for whom the Greek word is *pto-chós,* are the truly poor.[14] They have nothing and can get nothing by their own labor. They and they alone, in the New Testament, are presented as proper recipients of systematic charitable giving simply because they are poor.[15]

Some finer distinctions may be made between the second and third classes, and there are several other words sometimes used in the New Testament, as well as several in the Old, to designate the poor and the laboring classes, in addition to words and usages having to do not with economic but with social, legal, or spiritual status.

Some Practical Implications of a Biblical Definition of Poverty

Is all of this mere theoretical quibbling about words? Far from it. It has profound practical and moral implications.

First, it results in considerably lower estimates of the numbers of truly poor people, and thus of the numbers of people in need of (and legitimate recipients of) systematic charitable aid. And what is the advantage of this? Many people believe poverty is such an overwhelmingly huge problem that it can never be solved and that only governments have enough resources to do anything significant about it. A Biblical definition of poverty destroys those impressions and so can encourage people to undertake the truly effective, truly compassionate voluntary, private measures to combat poverty—measures like those that dominated America's responses to poverty in the nineteenth century and are vividly described in Marvin Olasky's outstanding book *The Tragedy of American Compassion.*[16]

As an example of this effect, consider poverty in the United States. When I wrote *Prosperity and Poverty,* my own studies led me to believe that the number of the poor in the United States, defined Biblically, was at most about 75 percent of that claimed in official government statistics (based on a relative definition of poverty).[17] (For simplicity's sake, I suggested defining only—but all—of the homeless as Biblically poor. In fact, many American homeless live well above mere subsistence, so the real poverty rate in America is certainly considerably lower even than this.) The official estimates—roughly 30 million, or 13 percent of the population[18]—create the impression of a problem insuperably large relative to non-governmental financial resources.[19] But if the number of the poor is really only 75 percent of that—about 250,000 or 1 percent of the population—it becomes clear that churches alone have more than enough resources to care fully for all of the truly poor in the United States. If more Christians were aware of this and took seriously the Bible's instructions to them regarding their responsibility to the poor, churches could reclaim the job of poor relief from the federal, state, and local governments in America.

Second, adopting this Biblical definition of poverty leads to a new understanding of what aid to the poor should target. Rather than targeting to raise the income of the poor above the "poverty level" as defined relative to GNP per capita, the immediate goal of poor *relief* is to raise them above mere subsistence, to make them no longer destitute.

This aim, along with the conclusion that what the Bible means by material poverty is actual destitution, finds support from the Apostle Paul's extended discussion of poverty relief in 1 Timothy 5–6. Near the conclusion of that study (6:8), Paul writes, ". . . if we have food and covering, with these we shall be content." Seen in context, this means that anyone who has food and covering (the latter reasonably implying both clothing and shelter adequate to protect one from the elements, which will differ from place to place and from season to season) is not truly poor (*ptochós*), and therefore not a proper recipient of systematic aid (although he might receive spontaneous aid).

No doubt, taking Paul's language here seriously means major adjustments in the notions of contentment, entertained by residents of the modern industrialized world who are accustomed to viewing as *necessities* what their forebears would have viewed as outrageous luxuries. It also deeply undermines the envy that presently drives much of the political debate and policy in the world, particularly in America. But we really must face squarely the question whether the world's current (and always changing) standards or the Bible's permanent standards are going to rule our thinking.

I will never forget the response to these ideas from Dr. Remenyi at Oxford. When I told him I thought the federally defined poverty level in the United States was too high and that a Biblical definition would categorize far fewer people as poor, he was incredulous. "But I've *lived* in the United States," he said, "while doing graduate studies, and you [he meant even a single person] simply cannot survive on less than $10,000 per year." Imagine his surprise when I told him that my wife and I and our three children had been living on less than $7,000 per year for each of the past four years, had never sought or accepted any form of government handouts, yet had never lacked adequate food, clothing, shelter, medical care, transportation, entertainment, or anything else—and had always considered ourselves abundantly blessed! What we can "live" on depends to a considerable extent on our choices about how we are going to live.

Third, adopting this definition of poverty carries a risk—a risk to our reputations. We will, no doubt, be accused of having no compassion on needy people. And in our age of absolute moral relativism, compassion has nearly become the only (other) absolute.

Yet we need not shrink back for fear of this risk. For, as economist Walter Williams put it in his devastating critique of institutionalized compassion toward his race, *The State Against Blacks,* ". . . truly compassionate policy requires dispassionate analysis."[20] When, as it is today, compassion is transmuted into mere pity, estranged from prudent examination of causes and effects, divorced from the intimate personal relationships that once characterized efforts to aid the poor, wedded to a cold, institutionalized welfare state with all its abuses and inefficiencies,[21] and made synonymous with the drive toward equality in the name of a perverted justice[22] there is little merit in being "compassionate."

Furthermore, when we consider what compassion really is—feeling something with someone—it becomes clear that it is in tying compassion to the relative definition of poverty that we create an unequal yoke. For if we take Paul seriously when he says we should be content if we have food and covering, then we must realize that the call to have compassion for the relatively but not truly poor *because of their "poverty"*—not for some other reasons—is chiefly the call to feel with them the discontent, the envy, the jealousy that our society so systematically and vociferously urges them to feel. There is nothing virtuous in sharing another's envy. There is, however, much virtue in feeling with another the suffering of real poverty.

Indeed, I venture to assert that it is precisely their instinctive sense that there is something wrong with calling people poor who are, by historical and world standards, sufficiently fed, clothed, housed, educated, medicated, and entertained that keeps many Americans from feeling any strong compassion toward the relatively poor. Sadly, however, this sensible caution can breed unwarranted cynicism toward anyone called poor, thereby undermining the motivation needed to help the truly poor. Thus, adopting the Biblical definition of poverty is the starting point for restoring real and proper compassion.

Fourth, why is adopting this definition of poverty crucial for restoring proper compassion? Because it allows us to target our aid to the truly poor, where it belongs. People with incomes above subsistence are not truly poor; people with incomes below it are.[23] As I stated earlier, it is scandalous when an un-Biblical notion of poverty leads us to expend on people who have far more than what Paul says anyone should be content to have, what we should expend on those who are in danger of starving to death.

Fifth, recognizing poverty as actual destitution allows us to bring back an important Biblical incentive to responsible work in order to counteract the tendency of many people to adopt the counter-productive mentalities of the underclass—immediate gratification of desires, short-term perspective, failure to save, low priority on work, and so on. Paul commanded that those who refuse to work should not be permitted to eat (2 Thess. 3:10). In our day, they need hardly worry about eating; the welfare state ensures that they not only eat but also live in what can only be called luxury by historic—or developing-world—standards. But there is much to be said for the effect of simple hunger in instilling the virtue of hard work. "The laborer's appetite," Solomon wrote, "works for him; his hunger drives him on" (Pr. 16:26).

I well recall a time in 1980 when, having lost an office job, I searched for a similar job for several weeks. At last I ran out of food. Unwilling to accept unemployment compensation or welfare, I went without food for the next couple of days. My hunger drove me to lower my expectations about the kind of job I would accept, and I quickly found one driving a truck for a warehouse. It wasn't what I preferred, but it was honest work. Had I not become hungry, I could easily have continued searching for a more "suitable" job, when what God intended was that I learn the discipline of doing whatever work He put before me.

For the sake of the truly poor, then, let us return to a Biblical definition of poverty. Doing so will make it far easier to return to Biblical means of ministering to the poor.

PART III

ANOTHER
REFORMATION:
HISTORICAL MODELS

8. EARLIER PARADIGMS FOR WELFARE REFORM: THE REFORMATION PERIOD

David W. Hall

This summary of several recent studies, centering on Calvin, Luther, and Vives, illustrates a hauntingly remarkable consensus among earlier Biblical thinkers on the subject of caring for the poor. Although modern hubris is quick to ignore earlier eras, in fact the sixteenth century had in place some of the best principles and practices for real poverty relief. With a church-based model, these Reformation-era Christians could help us today if we would listen to their testimony and learn from their examples. For positive models, we might begin here to see welfare reformed.

In the late twentieth-century church the diaconate and diaconal ministries may and should differ in notable ways from the classical Reformed tradition, but the latter still serves as one useful touchstone. No changes of time or space can alter the crucial importance of having a special, permanent, ecclesiastical office charged with leading the congregation in the corporate expression of love for the neighbor, provided that church members do not assume everything can be left to the official deacons. An ecclesiastical diaconate is not the only way Christians publicly act on their conviction that the worship of God is necessarily followed by service to the neighbor. It is perhaps the key institutional witness to, and guide for, the commitment of the church as a body to God's suffering people, wherever and whoever they may be.[1]

A s our country has now entered into a debate over welfare reform, in a thorny topic such as the church's role in social welfare, anyone feels foolish to brave theories and suggestions—even if based on what appear to be firm conclusions—without feeling as if he or she is out on a limb. One of the stalwart assistants in mature reflection on a subject like this is the utilization of church history as a corroborating guide. Accordingly, I would like to present some of the principles and practices of welfare from a period of church history nearly five centuries ago. One assumption is that over even large periods of time, the human condition and social solutions are basically constant. Therefore, it is unwise to fail to benefit from what has successfully worked in other eras. Any welfare reform will be better off if informed by history. This study selects some of the best practice from three different traditions within orthodox Christian practice: the Calvinist, the Lutheran, and the Romanist. In the first tradition we will concentrate on the contribution to the diaconate from John Calvin, as well as other leaders from the reformed tradition. The second part of this study focuses on a northern European model derived from Luther and the early adherents to Lutheranism. And the third examination will be a summary of the work of Juan Luis Vives, a leader of the Roman Catholic amelioration of poverty. Of these three, the Calvinistic tradition from this era provided the most radical innovation and likely provided more influence in our own society. Thus, that tradition will be highlighted in more detail.

In a 1989 book, Jeannine Olson presented the reading public with a fine historical work entitled *Calvin and Social Welfare: Deacons and the Bourse Francaise.*[2] The Bourse Francaise was founded under the leadership of John Calvin sometime between 1536 and 1541 (exclusive of his Strassbourg exile years). Its primary design was to appease the suffering brought onto French residents who, while fleeing persecution in France, came to Geneva. It is estimated that in that single decade (1550–1560) some 60,000 refugees came through Geneva, a significantly large number, producing great social stress. Of definite assistance to the Bourse in its early years was the philanthropic contribution of monies from France (p. 24). Olson guides us in a study of Calvin's personal impact on the Reformation, particularly highlighting the enduring effect of Calvin on the freshly re-created institution of the diaconate.

It is significant that we begin our study not with abstract theoretical principles, but with a summary of the *praxis* in Calvin's welfare remediation. Olson says, "The Reformers also understood the importance of charitable institutions, the welfare not only of the totally indigent and disadvantaged, but also of the many victims of the historical events of their times. Thus, within the organizational structure for charity in Geneva, the Bourse Francaise was a fundamental institution that cared not only for many humble refugees and the poor of Geneva, but also for French refugees of importance and consequence" (pp. 11–12). The "institutional organization of charity" was one of the contributions of Calvin to Western civilization: "The Bourse Francaise with its deacons became a fundamental institution in Calvin's Geneva alongside the disciplinary body of the Consistory with its elders and the ministerial association of the Venerable Company of Pastors" (p. 12). Olson is astute in pointing out that Calvin's welfare approach was in harmony with the other sixteenth-century attempts at welfare reform initiated by progressive humanists.[3]

Olson is also helpful in noting that the welfare program of Geneva was contoured to the theological emphases of the reformers, providing an earlier illustration that welfare practice was, and is, erected upon definite principles of religious or ideological nature. Moreover, the theology of the Reformation was the guiding force for this welfare, just as the theology of medieval Roman Catholicism was its guiding principle for almsgiving. Olson says, "Protestants emphasized charity as a response of love to God and one's neighbor" (p. 12). Ultimate principles contour the practice of welfare 450 years ago as today, which is to say, that at no time is welfare truly divorced from underlying ideological values.

Of course, the Genevan model for welfare did not claim uniqueness; it rather asserted itself as the culmination of a number of factors. It saw itself built upon the earlier precedents of the Levitical code (p. 18), as well as in strict continuity to the *Acts* narratives describing the work of the diaconate. Further, the development of the Genevan model by the church followed the train of the "Synod of Tours [which earlier] in 567 made each parish responsible for the poor dependent upon it charging its priest and budget for the welfare of the indigent" (p. 18). It was the Knights of St. John Hospitaller who began to minister to many of the health needs of the poor, and as early as 806 Charlemagne "had forbidden giving alms to lazy beggars circulating through his countryside" (p. 23). Thus, the Bourse saw itself as a historical continuation, standing on the shoulders of the work of Christians who had gone before.

The activities of the Bourse were numerous. Its diaconal agents were involved in housing orphans, the elderly, or those who were in any way incapacitated. They sheltered the sick, and dealt with orphans as well as those involved in immoralities. As precursors of voluntary societies in the nineteenth and twentieth century, attempts to "laicize" (p. 21) the work of the church made it more decentralized than a state-sponsored welfare.

Early on in the *Ecclesiastical Ordinances,* first proposed in 1541, John Calvin wrote a charter for the deacons, distinguishing them as one of the four basic offices. This early church order stipulated that among the fourth Biblical office, that of deacon, "There were always two kinds in the ancient Church, the one deputed to receive, dispense, and hold goods for the poor, not only daily alms, but also possessions, rents and pensions; the other to tend and care for the sick and administer allowances to the poor."[4] In addition, this charter prescribed, "It will be their duty to watch diligently that the public hospital is well maintained, and that this be so both for the sick and the old people unable to work, widowed women, orphaned children and other poor creatures. The sick are always to be lodged in a set of separate rooms from the other people who are unable to work. . . . Moreover, besides the hospital for those passing through which must be maintained, there should be some attention given to any recognized as worthy of special charity."[5] In conclusion of this section, Calvin advocated "to discourage mendicancy which is contrary to good order, it would be well, and we have so ordered it, that there be one of our officials at the entrance of the churches to remove from the place those who loiter; and if there be any who give offence or offer insolence to bring them to one of the Lords Syndic."[6] Begging without honest work was an affront to the Biblical Protestant work ethic from the earliest period. With sophistication of administration and discrimination of root causes among physical needs, this model can still inform our practice today.

Calvin was so interested in seeing the diaconate flourish that even "one of the elections of these deacons in fact, occurred at Calvin's house" (p. 27). Moreover in his will, Calvin not only left an inheritance for his family, but for the Boys School and poor strangers, as well.[7] In caring not only for refugees, but for many, Olson points out the important role of the deacons in establishing the Bourse: "In reality, the deacons cared for virtually every type of poor person, including those who spent the rest of their lives on welfare. On one end of the budget were the passersby who received a small sum adequate for an overnight stay, and on

the other end of the welfare spectrum were the aged, the
disabled, and the terminally ill who had no hope of becoming self-supporting. Between these two extremes
were a substantial variety" (p. 38). Thus did the deacons
care for a large range, not wholly dissimilar to the strata
of welfare needs in our own society.

In the 1541 *Ecclesiastical Ordinances* of Geneva,
Calvin recommended a strong role for the diaconate, especially in almsgiving. After two decades, those *Ecclesiastical Ordinances* were revised in 1561. A recent
translation[8] shows the sophistication and refinement of
the diaconate, even before the death of Calvin. The following sections, taken from the 1561 revision, make
clear that ministry to the poor was significant and well
ordered in Calvin's time. It was neither a low priority,
nor slip-shod in organization. The Swiss and French Reformed churches were agreed on "The Fourth Order of
the Ecclesiastical Government, the Deacons," which
were chartered as follows in the 1561 revision:

> 56. There were always two kinds in the ancient church:
> some delegated to receive, dispense and conserve the
> goods of the poor, daily alms as well as possessions, allow-
> ances, and pensions; others to attend to and care for the
> sick and administer the daily pittance.

> 60. It will be necessary to watch carefully that the common
> hospital is well maintained and that it is as much for the
> sick as for the elderly who are unable to work, such as
> widows, young orphans, and other poor. However, the sick
> shall be kept together in a lodging apart and separated from
> the others.

> 64. Let the ministers and commissioners or elders with one
> of the Syndics take the responsibility for inquiring whether
> in the above-mentioned administration of the poor there be

any fault or indigence. . . . And to do this, some of their company with the stewards shall visit the hospital quarterly to ascertain whether all is in good order.

65. It will also be necessary for the poor of the hospital as well as those of the city who have no way of helping themselves to have a doctor and a qualified surgeon on the city's payroll who, . . . were nevertheless engaged to care for the hospital and visit the other poor.

66. And because not only the old and sick are taken to our hospital but also young children because of their poverty, we have ordered that there always be a teacher to instruct them in morality, and in the rudiments of the letters and Christian doctrine. For the most part, he shall catechize, teaching the servants of the aforesaid hospital and conduct the children to the college.

In addition to maintaining a "hospital for infectious diseases, [which] shall be entirely separate, especially if the city happens to have been visited by some scourge from God," the deacons were also to discourage mendicancy: "Moreover, to prevent begging, which is contrary to good order, it will be necessary . . . that the Synod station some of its officers at the exits of the churches to remove those who would like to beg, and if they resist or are recalcitrant to take them to one of the trustees."

Olson continues and highlights the aim of supporting a productive work ethic:

The goal of the deacons was apparently to get able-bodied refugees back on their feet as soon as possible, providing temporary housing, short-term support, and job re-training when necessary. The deacons paid for tools to set up artisans in trade and provided some of them with raw materials. Cards were purchased for carders of wool, for example in woodworking tools for a woodworker. Such relatively

modest expenditures could make people financially independent with little outlay and since loans were preferred to
handouts, the deacons had an opportunity to recover some
of their outlay. Occasionally the Bourse advanced larger
sums, paying the rent for a shop of someone in business,
for instance. Disbursements to an individual were often
occasioned by a special recommendation of the owner or a
pastor. (p. 39)

Moreover, Olson notes the requirements of support
from these welfare agencies as follows: "At times the
deacons appeared to have encouraged people to leave in
order to relieve the welfare roles" (p. 40). Their goal was
to help those in need gain successful employment and to
hence dignify work. Yet Olson notes, "Of course not
every one who came wanted to work, and the city tried to
protect itself and the Bourse by requiring that newcomers
register their professional craft and the names of those
who would witness for them. This ordinance of 7 December 1568 also stipulated that no more people would be
received who were without profession or craft" (p. 40).
Thus, within a generation of this welfare work, the diaconate of Geneva discovered the need to communicate to
recipients the front-end goal and desire that they return to
work. "Despite frustration," Olson says, there were "some
refugees who did not want to work, [and] adult males
with marketable skills were relatively easy for the Bourse
to handle" (p. 40). Olson is commonsensical as well as
helpful, when she says that one of the "most promising
positive solutions for widows was remarriage" (p. 42),
noting that there were long-term solutions in mind.

Amidst all of this there were cases of abandonment,
reminiscent of our own contemporary problem of massive abandonment of child support. The Bourse was frequently called upon to raise children. They supported

those who were terminally ill who also left their children to be supported. "Subsistence payments, gifts of clothing, and medical bills were regularly recorded after the children's name" (p. 43). But all in all, "the Bourse's goal for these orphans was to provide them with a means of making a living and to get them out into the work-a-day world" (p. 43). At times even the "donors to the fund helped provide employment" (p. 43), foreshadowing a type of workfare that we may be rediscovering today. The Bourse included a ministry to widows often with dependent children and those with a variety of needs. Reflective of their view of welfare, for example, the Bourse paid for "shoe repairs . . . a variety of services and individual purchases, such as the laundering of a shirt and a basket for a small boy" (p. 46).

Still, however, it must be noted that although the Bourse resembled many other contemporary welfare funds, it had its own peculiarities. Of course there were theological peculiarities, but moreover these theological distinctives led to certain practical commitments. For example, "Apparently there was no regular handout of bread" (p. 45). Furthermore—as it will be noted later— there were certain prerequisites to receiving care with the possibility that certain moral deficiencies would annul the rights to be assisted by the Bourse.

The Bourse was not concerned only with spiritual or internal needs. On many occasions they hired medical doctors to take care of the ill. The records even "occasionally reveal the nature of the medical care, because sometimes the accountant specified what type of service was offered" (p. 46). Further, "the deacons hired guardians for those who were ill or disabled and provided for their dependence. The deacons arranged for the care of the sick, at first in private homes and inns and later in the city hospital" (p. 46), reflecting the full scope of diaconal ministry not being limited only to evangelism. Those who led the Bourse were also prudent. By January of 1581, the Bourse adopted a set of constitutional rules (pp. 104–106), underscoring the need to have a vital and well-thought-out, disciplined approach to poverty amelioration.

For our own times, it is perhaps instructive to note that in Calvin's era social welfare was not totally egalitarian. Olson notes,

> There was an effort in Geneva to maintain the image of the Bourse Francaise as a fund to help people who were considered worthy, rather than as an institution that indiscriminately aided everyone. The funds were intended for those who were in genuine need, particularly those who were ill or handicapped. The deserving poor were numerous in this age before modern medicine or surgery, when a simple hernia or poorly aligned broken bone could render one unable to work. The limited funds of the Bourse were not intended for derelict poor, those who are considered unwilling to work, lazy and slothful vagrants and vagabonds, to use the popular English terminology of the era. The assumption that welfare recipients should be worthy of aid had long been common in Europe, but the definition of worthiness varied from one milieu to another. (p. 139)

As Olson and others note, "Despite the distinction between the deserving and the derelict poor, the deacons were sometimes accused of being overly generous and hesitant to turn anyone away" (p. 139); so did charity motivate these to err on the side of charity. Still, however, there were times and instances in the records of the Bourse when the deacons would not give assistance to those because of attitudinal or moral blights. Charity did not imply a style of giving which nullified personal industry and responsibility. Their definition of worthiness apparently consisted, "Of a healthy blend of religious conviction, humility, appreciativeness, and good behavior, in addition to genuine need, of course" (p. 140). There were a number of instances in which if one were to behave immodestly or unchastely, he would not receive certain aid. In short, "Welfare recipients were definitely expected to maintain certain standards of acceptable behavior" (p. 140). Indeed on occasion, "The Bourse withdrew aid for a while" (p. 142), if those receiving its dole would not conform their behavior to Christian ethics. Moreover, it must be reiterated that "The deacons also tried to keep those who were already on the welfare roles in line" (p. 143). The deacons, as agents of private religious charity, did definitely attempt, according to Olson, to use the Bourse as a means of discipline, moral influence, and incentive for productivity.

In his *Commentaries,* Calvin also consistently puts forth similar principles. On 2 Thessalonians 3:10 which says "If anyone will not work, he shall not eat," Calvin comments, "When, however, the Apostle commanded that such persons should not eat, he does not mean that he gave commandment to those persons, but forbade that the Thessalonians should encourage their indolence by supplying them with food. . . . Paul censures those lazy drones who lived by the sweat of others, while they contribute no service in common for aiding the human race."[9] Commenting on Psalms 112:9, the Genevan reformer says:

> By dispersing [to the poor], the prophet intimates that they did not give sparingly and grudgingly, as some do who imagine that they discharge their duty to the poor when they dole out a small pittance to them, but that they give

liberally as necessity requires and their means allow; for it may happen that a liberal heart does not possess a large portion of the wealth of this world . . . they give to the poor, meaning that they do not bestow their charity at random, but with prudence and discretion meet the wants of the necessitous. We are aware that unnecessary and superfluous expenditure for the sake of ostentation is frequently lauded by the world; and consequently, a larger quantity of the good things of this life is squandered away in luxury and ambition than is dispensed in charity prudently bestowed. The prophet instructs us that the praise which belongs to liberality does not consist in distributing our goods without any regard to the objects upon whom they are conferred, and the purposes to which they are applied, but in relieving the wants of the really necessitous.[10]

These founders of this Genevan Diaconate were "Neither reactionaries nor social revolutionaries in the modern sense. They were unaware that they were setting precedents for social welfare and philanthropy that would endure" (p. 17). Thus, the experiment in welfare in Geneva offers to us a clinic in what may happen without a great deal of thought, but by reacting with primarily Biblical instincts.

It is helpful to remember also that the Bourse Francaise was a hinge institution. Occurring at the consummation of centuries of medieval welfare as rarified by the Protestant Reformation, these founders of the Bourse Francaise, "Did not believe that poverty could be entirely eliminated but this did not immobilize them" (p. 17). In reference to Jesus' statement in Mark 14:7 that we "always have the poor with you," these founders of the Genevan Diaconate were humanists who "looked to ancient Greece and Rome for their models for the present. As Reformers they were most attracted to the institution of the early church. They found precedent therein for much of what they did" (p. 17). So they lived on an ebb of a reformed movement, nonetheless looking to what had gone before them. Olson says, "They were looking to the past and the present rather than to the future."

As those who look to the past, in comparison with the inadequacies of the present, perhaps we too should share some of that posture. We might be better off from this and other studies to see what we can learn from the past, rather than looking chiefly to the future. In fact, if we find ourselves advocating practices markedly different from what the Bourse in Geneva did nearly five centuries ago, then we might argue that if their practices had any merit at all as far as systemic assistance to welfare, then we must ask if our departure from their proven and tested methods should not be suspect.

Emphasizing the value of historical studies, Elsie McKee in *Diakonia in the Classical Reformed Tradition and Today* confirms:

> Before one can reform or even evaluate some part of life, whether individual or corporate, it is important to understand how present practices developed. What other ages have taught and done is not necessarily normative for the twentieth century, but failure to understand what we have inherited can make us puppets of the unknown past. It can also deny us the gifts of the faith and the wisdom of the communion of the saints.[11]

Moreover, McKee's own independent study corroborates the previously noted "work ethic," as she explains:

> From this Protestant viewpoint, Roman Catholic almsgiving to healthy beggars who could work seemed indiscriminate; it was not charity but irresponsible stewardship. The new valuation of work—not as a means of earning or even

proving salvation but as an expression of gratitude and responsible use of God-given talents—was clearly a critical factor in the prohibition of begging among Protestants.[12]

In her more thorough and quite scholarly treatment *John Calvin on the Diaconate and Liturgical Almsgiving*,[13] Elsie Anne McKee notes the emphasis on the role of the diaconate in ministering to the poor in Calvin's thought, as follows:

> The portion of John Calvin's ecclesiology known as the office of the diaconate is, paradoxically, a doctrine as important as it is neglected. The modern Reformed tradition suffers ecclesiologically for this amnesia, but the importance of this doctrine is glimpsed also in scholarly controversies agitating other disciplines of modern research. . . . Not infrequently, Calvin—or rather, fragments of Calvin— figure in one or another of these scholarly debates. However accurately quoted the fragments may be, they sometimes make limited theological sense because their full context is not seen or at least not made clear. . . . despite the relative lack of emphasis on it, Calvin's teaching on the diaconate is a coherent and not insignificant theological development. Studied alongside his equally neglected views on liturgical almsgiving, this doctrine answers apparently diverse questions by showing their mutual relationships within the single doctrine of the Church; its development also contributes to a richer understanding of Reformed ecclesiology. (p. 13)

Much of McKee's treatise includes numerous primary references to other contemporary reformers whose writings reveal a mainline, consensual teaching on the need and Scripturalness of the office of deacon ministering to the poor. McKee notes, for example, that John a Lasco's *Forma ac ratio* actually associates the final benediction with the collection of alms by deacons stationed at the doors of the church: "Then, a psalm having been sung, the whole church is dismissed in peace by the preacher, with the commendation of the poor and the blessing, in these words: 'Remember your poor and let each in turn pray for the others. And may God have mercy on you and bless you. May the divine countenance shed His light upon you for the glory of His holy name, and keep you in His holy and saving peace. Amen.' " A Lasco's liturgy further specified:

> When, however, these things are said by the preacher, the deacons according to their turns place themselves in order at the doors of the church, and after the church is dismissed, they diligently collect alms at the very doors of the church, and immediately they write down whatever they have collected, in the church itself. Moreover, this is also customarily always observed in all other gatherings of the church. (p. 40)

Moreover, as McKee notes, the same was "also the practice in the order of service used by Martin Micronius in London (1554) and Eastfriesland (1565). In a brief pamphlet (1551), Peter Paul Vergerio describes the worship of the London Strangers' Church, apparently a Lasco's liturgy, which associates the final blessing with a collection at the door" (pp. 40–41).

Even Phillippe Mornay, at the end of the century, describes the practice of the Reformed community in France, as set out in the church order proposed at Poitiers in 1557: "The collection for the poor shall be made at each preaching, at the end, and the said collection shall be written down by the hand of the minister on the paper of the deacons and kept by the said deacons to be placed in the hands of the treasurer on the day of the consistory meeting (p. 41).

Calvin, in a sermon on 1 Timothy 3:8–10, associates the early church's compassion as the canon to measure our "Christianity": "When there were neither lands nor possessions nor what is called property of the church, it was necessary that each give his offering and from that the poor be supplied. If we want to be considered Christians and want it to be believed that there is some church among us, this organization must be demonstrated and maintained" (p. 62). Later in that same sermon he enjoined, "Now when that property has been distributed as it ought, if that still does not meet all needs, let each give alms privately and publicly, so that the poor may be aided as is fitting (p. 62).

The testimony of Calvin is quite full. In one of his sermons on 1 Timothy 3:8–13, he remarked,

> We saw this morning what position St. Paul discusses here, that is, that of those who in the ancient church were ordained to distribute the alms. It is certain that God wants such a rule observed in His church: that is, that there be care for the poor—and not only that each one privately support those who are poor, but that there be a public office, people ordained to have the care of those who are in need so that things may be conducted as they ought. And if that is not done, it is certain that we cannot boast that we have a church well-ordered and according to the Gospel, but there is just so much confusion. (p. 183)

Later, in the same source, Calvin would comment, "And yet the deacons are those ordained to have the care of the poor and to distribute alms, the care not only of distributing what is entrusted to them, but of inquiring where there is need and where the property ought to be used," and "We must find people who may govern the property of the poor. These are the sacrifices offered to

God today, that is, alms. Therefore it is necessary that they be distributed by those whom God considers suitable for such a position, and that the deacons who are chosen should be as the hands of God, and be there in a holy office" (p. 184).

So strong was Calvin's view that he preached,

> Inasmuch as it is a question of the spiritual government which God has put among His own, St. Paul wants those who are ordained, whether to proclaim the Gospel or to have the care of the poor, to be of irreproachable life . . . We must carefully note these passages where it is proclaimed to us what order God has established in His Church, so that we may take care to conform ourselves to it the best we can . . . Because if we want to have the Church among us, we must have this government which God has established as inviolable, or at least we must strive to conform ourselves to it. (p. 184)

Calvin, whose name is not always and immediately identified with passionate advocacy for welfare to the poor, even on one occasion rhetorically asserted, "Do we want to show that there is reformation among us? We must begin at this point, that is, there must be pastors who bear purely the doctrine of salvation, and then deacons who have the care of the poor (p. 184).

McKee summarizes the Genevan practice as follows:

> Two or three things about most Protestants' almsgiving are notably different from the late medieval equivalent. One is the new organization, the coordination and centralization. This, however, was common to Roman Catholic as well as Protestant charity, and became universal. Another point is the matter of the poor begging for alms, whether in church or in the streets. . . . Protestants permitted only designated people to collect alms for the poor. . . . A third point, however, the fact that Protestant almsgiving was repeat-

edly, explicitly or implicitly associated with the central official act of worship, distinguishes it from sixteenth century Roman Catholicism as well as from the late medieval church. Among the great majority of the Reformed churches, an alms collection became part of the regular worship order. . . . At least for the Reformed tradition, an adequate understanding of the relationship of worship and benevolence can be more fully, perhaps, better, achieved by an investigation of the diaconate . . . the doctrine of the diaconate . . . determines the ecclesiastical or civil nature of charity in the sixteenth century. (p. 65)

The emphases of Calvin lived on after his death. Even Jean Morely, one of the adversaries of Calvin's disciple Theodore Beza, affirmed a strong role for the church to care for those in poverty. In his 1562 *Treatise on Christian Discipline,* Morely asserted that the church, in some organized manner should "relieve the poor, and property should be set aside for its support. For poverty creates temptations to vice and corruption which few can resist . . . many of the arrangements are designed primarily to keep the able-bodied but indolent poor from receiving aid on a regular basis, so that all the church's resources for poor relief can go to those victims of circumstance who are deserving and helpless."[14]

Of all the reformers, still it is Martin Bucer who is considered the "theologian of the diaconate," as he writes most directly about the function of the church in caring for the poor. Bucer argued in his 1560 *De Regno Christi* that, "there must be in the 'Christian Republic' a thorough organization of poor relief and assistance to the sick . . . for the fulfillment of these ends discipline is essential, and so there must be a thorough organization of labour and leisure."[15]

For a slightly fuller description of Bucer's view of the diaconate, Basil Hall records:

> "Deacons are joined to the ministry of bishops and presbyters to minister to them and especially to care for the poor," he wrote in his commentary on Ephesians 4 . . . that "the officium *et munus* of Deacons . . . is for the sustaining of the poor. . . . Private men, great or small in condition, must contribute to the work of God in the Churches, both from their immovable and movable goods . . . [the Deacons are] diligently to distribute from this to all the poor in the Church, whether local people or strangers.

Bucer goes so far as to say of the diaconate that "without it there can be no true communion of saints,"[16] while simultaneously believing that,

> The first duty of the deacons is to distinguish between the deserving and undeserving poor, for the former to inquire carefully into their needs; the latter, if they lead disorderly lives at the expense of others, to expel them from the community of the faithful. Care, next, is to be taken for needy widows. The second duty of deacons is to keep a written record of accounts, having sought diligently for the proper collecting of funds from all the parishioners.[17]

John Knox continued this reformation tradition of ministry to the poor in Scotland. For example, in the *Second Book of Discipline* (1578), the Scottish emphasis can be seen from the following stipulations, codified in the Scottish book of government (chapter VIII), in which the office of Deacon is concerned "to collect and distribute the whole ecclesiastical goods unto those to whom they are appointed."[18]

Earlier, the Scots Confession (1560), in chapter 28 had stipulated:

Now the true use of the ecclesiastical goods was, and now is, to maintain learning in schools and in holy assemblies, with all the service, rites, and buildings of the Church; finally, to maintain teachers, scholars, and ministers, with other necessary things, and *chiefly for the succor and relief of the poor* (emphasis added). . . . Therefore, we teach that schools and colleges whereunto corruption is crept in doctrine, in the service of God, and in manners, must be reformed; and that there provision should be made, piously, faithfully, and wisely for the relief of the poor.

Hence, the Calvinistic tradition was firm and fairly uniform in their institutionalization of the care for the poor. It was an ecclesiological function to be carried out by spiritual officers according to Biblical standards and principles. As it was carried out well, it cared for the poor, employed the church's gifts, encouraged a productive work ethic, and predated (relieved) governmental stewardship in this area. As Bromiley summarizes:

The able-bodied should work and support themselves. . . . The answer to poverty was still found in individual benevolence exercised either privately or through the Church. The Reformers themselves all set good examples in this regard. Luther, although he claimed that "God does not want you to give to needy people in such a way that you and yours must also beg and be a burden to other people," was, in fact, generous almost to the point of improvidence. . . . Apart from private gifts, the care of the sick and needy was a responsibility of the parish."[19]

Luther in Germany

Martin Luther, the other magisterial reformer, also translated his faith into practice in the area of poverty relief. As early as 1520, in his *Address to the German Nobility,* Luther "strongly disapproved of any and every kind of mendicancy and beggary and advised every town to assume responsibility for its own poor and needy by appointing an official to advise the pastor."[20] Begging was to be eliminated, in part as its erstwhile theological foundation crumbled under Dr. Luther's *sola fides* theology. Begging could no longer be viewed as a monastic ideal, as meritorious works, nor as Christian perfection. Instead, it was to be curtailed as much as possible by a proper theological correction, in lieu of the Romanist approach. Begging would then be eradicated by being lodged as the responsibility of each small unit of governing, the individual cities. In his *Babylonian Captivity* (1520) Luther saw the church through its diaconate as the agency to minister to the poor, in contrast to the role of deacons in Roman Catholicism: "The diaconate . . . is a ministry, not for reading the Gospel and the Epistle, as the practice is nowadays, but for distributing the Church's bounty to the poor, in order that the priests might be relieved of the burden of temporal concerns and give themselves more freely to prayer and the Word."[21] In Strassburg, "we find as early as 1523 a thorough evangelical organization under the care of a director, four assistant directors, nine church workers with twenty-one helpers. Here it was stipulated that the poor were not only to be helped materially but to be visited as persons at least four times in a year."[22] Ministry to the poor by the church was not a later development for the reformers.

In a study of Lutheranism, a few outstanding cities are both exemplary and reflective of the value of Lutheran welfare. In 1522, in Wittenberg, Luther helped sponsor a church ordinance that provided for a common chest to assist the poor. Again, Olson is helpful in describing Lutheran practice:

The phrase common chest referred to a cash fund for the poor with all the property that stood behind it. Often an actual chest was locked with several keys, which were distributed among several responsible people to insure the security of the properties, incomes, monies, writes, and goods of the chest. Perishables, such as food were kept elsewhere. The common chest was funded both by current donations and by property inherited from the pre-Reformation period. In Wittenberg this included property from the church, confraternities, and endowments. (p. 161)[23]

It would be a gross error to fail to comprehend the theological rooting of the practice of *diaconia* bedded firmly in Luther's conception of justification by faith. As James Atkinson has observed,

It is important to bear in mind that Luther's teaching on *diaconia* was the sequel of a precise theological formulation. It was neither a return to the ways of the primitive Church of Acts, nor was it an attempt to cope with the immense social problem of beggary maintained by catholic merit-earning practice. In effect it did restore primitive convictions and practice, and it also, by its teaching on justification by faith, caused works as a means of grace to wither away and work as a means of grace to rehabilitate itself. Nevertheless these were only fruits of a profound theological revolution.[24]

These poverty-relief ministries were consistent outgrowths of theoretical bases. Shortly thereafter, Luther also helped establish a form of diaconal welfare through Karlstadt as Wittenberg drew up an "Ordinance for a common purse dividing the cities into four quarters each with a trusted citizen disbursing the welfare in those quarters" (p. 162). Eleven years later, by 1533, the ordinance for the diaconate was even more formal, although it was broadened to include the funding of ministers. In another city, Leiznig, Luther's influence on welfare can be seen. A common chest was established as well with ten trustees in which the disbursements were to be made after weekly meetings of the board on the Lord's Day (p. 162). In Leiznig, "The common chest supported the poor living in their homes, cared for and fed orphans, apprenticed and educated children, provided dowries for marriageable girls, and lent money to worthy artisans and merchants. Luther also suggested that the citizens of Leiznig establish schools for boys and girls in monastery buildings" (p. 163).

Martin Luther, in the *Church Order of Brunswick,* 1528, stressed the following:

> In all large parishes there shall openly stand a Common Chest for the indigent, the poor, and others in need. To it shall come all free-will offerings which men shall put therein throughout the year, as each is disposed; . . . whatever pious Christian people can devise for the help of these chests shall belong thereto; item, the Deacons of the Poor shall . . . go round on holydays before and after the sermon in church with bags whereon shall be a little bell so that they need not ask but that the people shall hear that they are there . . . and preachers shall in their sermons recommend such service of the poor as Divine Service . . . For these chests there shall be chosen three Deacons by the Council and by the members of the Commune in the district . . . The Deacons shall keep an account of their receipts and expenditure, and a list of the names and houses of those who from week to week are in need of assistance, so that their reckoning may be the simpler and clearer. . . . Every Sunday, or other appointed day in the week, the Deacons shall meet together in each parish to distribute to the poor according to need, and to consider what is necessary for each sick or poor man.[25]

In another part of Luther's Germany, in Nuremberg, perhaps the most famous system of Lutheran welfare systems was developed. So famous was Nuremberg for its social approach that even the catholic humanist Juan Louis Vives sought to imitate many of its principles. Further, "Emperor Charles the Fifth asked for a draft of the Nuremberg welfare legislation before issuing his own 1531 ordinance, the adoption of which he then urged on the cities of the low countries" (p. 163). Reform in Nuremberg actually commenced as early as 1522 with a complete system of relief for the poor being enacted by ordinance on July 24, 1522. At Nuremberg, the typically Lutheran collection boxes or cauldrons were put in places quite visible and near the church, with their funds to be distributed by the leaders of the respective communities.

Zurich also was a model for social welfare. The city began its reform and its diaconal ministry as early as 1520. The same may be said for Strassburg and other cities in Lutheran territory. For example, "In Strassburg, preaching of welfare reform began before the Protestant Reformation. Geiler Von Kaysersberg urged a new system of poor relief that included a suggestion that able-bodied people should work. Only those incapable of work, he argued, should receive relief" (p. 165). Remembering that Calvin, when exiled from Geneva, spent two years in the late 1530s in Strassburg, it is possible that these other Swiss Reformed models could have indeed shaped, in no small part, the welfare relief model of Geneva. Luther, it should also be remembered, was opposed to handouts without responsibility and true demonstration of need, as he earthily quipped, "Do not spoonfeed the masses. If we were to support Mr. Everybody, he would turn too wanton and go dancing on the ice."[26] The "poor by their own folly" were not deserving of help, according to Luther.

Besides requiring careful safeguards and an annual audit, Atkinson summarizes the Biblical principles in Martin Luther's welfare reform:

> Vagrant scroungers, the workshy, and ne'er-do-wells were treated with firmness: help was given, but only at minimum levels with the maximum of good counsel! The deacons were always predisposed to help or even to re-establish a genuine worker. There was always a remedial touch to their activities, and where a man was the victim of his own sin, careful consideration was given as to the reformation of his character and habits. Deacons were expected to know all their needy personally, and the unknown poor needed very respectable credentials to be helped. Poor folk genuinely travelling were helped (as residents), and were not classed as vagrants. It was generally accepted as normal practice that relatives should help their own, and each had a Christian responsibility to his own neighbour, apart from the official responsibility of the deacons.[27]

Yet lest the Lutheran approach be thought of as stingy, it has been observed,

> What is particularly impressive about this work is the real concern for the genuinely sick, particularly to women in childbirth. Careful allowances are given to midwives and to home help for the mother. Genuine solicitude is shown for the young, especially the neglected or orphaned. These children were schooled and trained for a trade. There is evidence of deacons asking the wealthy to pay school fees or further education fees for bright boys, and of this being considered an honourable and Christian request. The deacons helped the girls to an honourable marriage. Prisoners and delinquents, too, were given special care, and were visited and helped by the clergy: condemned prisoners

were to be given spiritual comfort and the sacrament offered them.[28]

From this we can see that a number of welfare agencies began to blossom in the countryside of Western Europe following the Protestant Reformation. Indeed, the Calvinistic diaconate was a leader in its manifestation of consistent reformation of faith and life. Olson concludes:

> Within the first generation of its founding, similar deacons funds were created by Reformed churches across the continent and in England. The parent institution in Geneva provided a model and an inspiration, keeping morale alive and offering a place of refuge to Reformed Christians faced with persecution and war and the increasingly foreboding world. The Bourse Francaise was a linchpin in the organizational structure of Reformed Churches providing financial links and strengthening the survival skills of that persistent minority the Reformed Church of early modern Europe. (p. 182)

Thus did these Reformation prototypes spread and become leaders in the sixteenth century welfare reform. Indeed, the Reformation "left stamped upon Christendom its idea of a properly co-ordinated and managed care of the poor and needy as the concern of the Church and as the responsibility of the Christian community."[29]

Vives: Late Medieval Roman Catholic Welfare

One can also profit by the example of the Roman Catholic humanist, Juan Luis Vives.[30] The major source of his views on social welfare may be found in his 1526 *On the Help of the Poor*. Vives, a product of renaissance humanism, offered a state-of-the-art, mature version of welfare. In that both Vives and the Protestant reformers had drunk deeply from the pedagogy of humanism, in some ways their systems resembled each other's.

Vives, respected in his day for a range of expertise, applied his talents to the remediation of poverty. He maintained views that may stand out in our own times, but to his contemporaries he was putting forth mere Christian charity. Vives wrote, "I will not have as a Christian he who, within his means, gives no help to an indigent brother."[31] For Vives, "The Christian society, the society which strives for earthly justice, looks to the divine law to be reconstituted as just, thus imitating the self's interaction with grace."[32] Alves and others even trace many of the poverty-relief laws enacted in Spain in the 1520s and 1530s to the influence of Vives on these matters. In fact, so decidedly Christian was Vives's method that he drew attack from the rival secularists who preferred to follow Machiavelli. Vives advocated the impact of the principles of Christian morality on welfare and believed that the "'lay' urban social organism was to be a reflection of Christian morality."[33] Along with Loyola, he affirmed the propriety of catechetical instruction as a part of any Christian-based welfare, along with the administration of fines to punish professional beggars.[34] He may even have predated by four and a half centuries Pope John XXIII who stressed the family basis of welfare as:

> The family, grounded on marriage freely contracted, monogamous and indissoluble, must be considered the first and essential cell of human society. To it must be given, therefore, every consideration of an economic, social, cultural, and moral nature which will strengthen its stability and facilitate the fulfillment of its specific mission.[35]

Vives's method is summarized by Alves:

The methods of his proposed system included a division of the poor into deserving native elements and undeserving foreign beggars; the establishment of work programs; and the generation of relief revenue through donations, the earnings of the poor's labor, and the use of money previously spent by the city on frivolous festivals. . . . poor relief necessarily resulted from the Christian organic concept, but the Christian social thinker knew in advance that the ideal would never function perfectly on earth. . . . Vives desired vocational training for young paupers so that they would not always remain impoverished, but he wanted to keep both able-bodied and handicapped adults actively employed at all times to prevent idleness, the devil's playground. Those who were so morally corrupt that they refused to work were to be given just enough food to stay alive; but they were still to be given food.[36]

Vives shared with Calvin and other Protestants the view of depravity which maintained that both the charity dispensers and the charity recipients were sinful, and hence, must be constrained by order and accountability. Furthermore, "Vives, Calvin, and Loyola all recognized the importance of planned relief. They distinguished between deserving and undeserving poor, and they all accepted the occasional confinement of the poor to hospitals as a given."[37]

Calvin, and later Beza, "condemned the unwillingness of the wealthy to aid the poor; with Calvin quite clearly stating that reluctance to work tried God's power and patience."[38] Loyola went so far as to construct a scale of punishments for able-bodied beggars, and as an example of the Roman Catholic approach of the time, he maintained that "Kindness and harsh discipline both [were needed] in actual Christian practices," and that based on the separation of the sheep from the goats in Matthew

25:40, "There had to be deserving and undeserving poor to explain this dichotomy. The sick, disabled, widowed, and orphaned were separated from the sturdy and lazy."[39] In fine, "Social control and social responsibility were interwoven."

The farthest thing from the minds of these social and religious reformers was the isolation of faith from practice. They believed that faith had every right to impose its own structure and discipline, even method, on religiously administered welfare. It was, after all, nonpublic and religious. As Alves points out, "social control was still based on principles of charity," and "Thus, poor relief and the reform of personal morals were never far from [their] minds as proper activities for the Christian in the world."[40] The only remaining differences between Catholic and Protestant welfare at the time were in terms of philosophic approach.

Vives, Calvin, Luther, Bucer, and Knox presented a rather consensual approach to the church's role in social welfare. They gave great credence to the metaphor of the body being organically related (1 Cor. 12), both poor and nonpoor. They reasoned, "Just as injury to the extremities can eventually harm the entire organism, so too prolonged hardship among the poor can feed the flames of civil disorder. When ignored, the poor generally rise up to demand satisfaction of their needs. Thus, *On the Help of the Poor* portrays poor relief as an important tool for the maintenance of social order and control, but it is also presented as a Christian duty with antecedents in classical thought."[41]

Hence, for the reformers of nearly five centuries ago, "The moral and spiritual health of the community was thus linked to such practical material concerns as poor relief. For Vives, Calvin, and Loyola, the obsession with the social organism myth and practical poor relief was not accidental. It was mimesis."[42] These welfare reformers looked to the past, specifically the canon of Scripture, to give the broad principles of social welfare. True, they did not expect of Scripture that every issue would be addressed by Scripture, but they did expect, and did find, the broad brushstrokes necessary for erecting a consistent and distinct Biblical approach to welfare. The Christian religion then established the most powerful and longest lasting welfare model of any in modern western civilization. Only conceit or bias would fail to consult this eminently successful model, to glean its enduring principles for our own times.

In sum, these consensual policy principles from the Reformation era could be summarized as:

- Welfare was only for the truly disadvantaged—a distinction between the deserving and the nondeserving poor was maintained. If one will not work, they will not be assisted (2 Thess. 3:10).

- Moral prerequisites properly accompanied assistance from religious (private) agencies.

- Welfare was via private or religious charity, not state largesse, with the family as the first rung of relief.

- Ordained officers managed and brought accountability.

- Theological underpinnings were normal and theology guided practice.

- A productive work ethic was sought, that is, welfare relief was temporary, with a long-term goal of industriousness involved.

- History is valuable in illuminating workable practices.

- Each church was to administer a "common chest," or diaconal outreach of some kind.

Sadly, over the centuries much of this ministry has been surrendered by the church. There are several possible reasons for the eclipse of diaconal ministry. Among them are changes in polity, pietism, and the expectations of statism.

Such a study as the above provides an historical foundation for those in modern times to compare, and from which to construct, future welfare reform. The future of welfare reform would do well to have history as its friend. To spurn this chief advisor is to condemn future reform to errors as great as the recent past. Perhaps its time to go backward. We could hardly do more damage. This time, let's let history have a seat at the roundtable.

9. AGAINST THE TIDE: FOUR ALTERNATIVE MOVEMENTS

George Grant

When seeking replacements for the failed societal policies of our day, George Grant identifies four other movements of the last century which may help in the reformulation of welfare. With the keen eye of a historian and the insights of a prophet, Grant introduces many readers to the thought of the Southern Agrarians, conservative Progressives, Kuyperians, and traditional distributionist Roman Catholics, as exemplified by Pope Leo XIII's Rerum Novarum. *Containing a mass of information in a short span, this thought-provoking essay provides seed-thoughts from proven and potential models for compassion in action.*

> *Christianity conceals in its womb a much greater treasure of rejuvenation than you surmise. Until now it has exerted its power only on the individual and only indirectly on the state. But anyone who, as believer or as unbeliever, has been able to spy out its secret dynamic, must grant that Christianity can exert a wonderful organizing power on society also; and not till this power breaks through will the religion of the cross shine before the whole world in all the depths of its conception and in all the wealth of the blessings which it brings.*[1]

*T*he dominating bathing beauty of modernity is *ideology*. It is the skin-deep facility of the systemologue. Like the beauty of the flesh—of celebrity, athleticism, suasion, and fashion—ideology's attractiveness is little more than a passing fancy. The grass withers, the flowers fade, and man's contrivances of socio-political contrivances—however beautiful—last but for a moment.

The smothering influence of ideology's adornment is everywhere evident. It seems to have worked its charms on and wrested control of every political party, of every nationalist movement, of every cultural trend, of every intellectual impulse, even of every religious revival in our time. From Nazism and Stalinism to Shi'itism and Humanism, from Pluralism and Multi-culturalism to Liberalism and Conservatism, from Bolshevism and Maoism to Monopolism and Socialism, ours has been a century of movements beguiled by the temporal seductions of ideology.

Nearly every question, every issue, and every social dilemma has been and continues to be translated into political, juridical, mechanical, structural, mathematical, or systemic terms. They are supplied with bureaucratic, mathematical, technological, or—hear the hush of reverential awe—scientific solutions. They are, in short, reduced to the lowest common denominator language of ideology.

Social reformer Jane Addams was hardly exaggerating when she said, "ideology is the modern ecology. It is the landscape we see, the sound we hear, the food we eat, the air we breathe. It is the incarnation of truth for us and the emblem and impress of earthly harmony. It is the essence of modern beauty."

Ideology and the Poor

As the twentieth century has unfolded, it has become increasingly evident that while all of us have been profoundly affected by ideology, its greatest affect has been upon the poor, the common, the forgotten, and the helpless—those Marx and Bakunin chose to dub the proletariat. For them, ideology's *das boot* has been fierce and unrelenting precisely because they do not fit easily into its systemic ideals. They are, to be truthful, an embarrassing inconvenience, to the utopian systemizers who have happily refined the reform process to five-year plans, eighty-page economic proposals, ethnic purges, or razzle-dazzle "United We Stand" campaigns. They have no place in the paradigmatic matrix of ideology.

That is why the poor have been so violently victimized even by their supposed champions in the twentieth century. "Of all the tyrannies," C. S. Lewis wrote, "a tyranny sincerely expressed for the good of its victims may be the most oppressive. It may be better to live under robber barons than under omnipotent ideological busybodies."

Thus, the underclasses have suffered in our time like never before. No century has been more comprehensively brutal, onerous, or despotic to what the Bible calls "the least of these." Not in ancient times when the poor were but chattel, not in the medieval epoch when the poor were but peasants, not in the emerging industrial age when the poor were but fodder for the engines of progress, not ever have they been so routinely, so universally, and so efficiently suppressed, stigmatized, and even slaughtered.

Ideology—whatever its stripe—is unsparing in its inhuman humanism. It always has been; it always will be.

Sadly, many of the sincere Christian attempts at ministering to the poor in our day have attempted to accommodate themselves to the prevailing ideological environment. These well-intentioned efforts view the problem of poverty through the tenured lens of modern economic and political systems. Though incidental aspects of this or that system may be questioned, the dominant worldview of the systemizers remains unchallenged: that *some* ideological system must be implemented. As a result, little is changed. The poor are tossed to and fro on the waves of doubtful premises and promises.

Years ago Russell Kirk argued that, "Because ideology is by essence anti-religious, Christians tend to be attracted to ideology's negation, Conservatism." But in our time, even Movement Conservatism has taken on the messianic aspirations of ideology—it has become a kind of amoral capitalistic shop-and-till prop for Monopolism or Mercantilism.

Christian Resistance

In the good providence of God, four movements within the broad sweep of Christendom foresaw this difficulty and challenged the emerging neo-orthodoxy of ideology. Though they seemed to come from the four ends of the earth temperamentally, philosophically, ecclesiastically, and geographically, they were all spawned in a single year with a single purpose: to demonstrate genuine Christian compassion, justice, and mercy to all men everywhere.

In 1891, the versatile and prolific Abraham Kuyper—known to all the world as a preacher-turned-journalist-turned-politician in the Netherlands—delivered a sterling address to the first Christian Social Congress entitled *The Social Problem and the Christian Religion*. Though it spawned decades of healthy debate and constructive activity, its greatest contribution was to ignite the worldwide political phenomenon of the *Christian Democrat Movement*.

In 1891, the brilliant and pious Vincenzo Gioacchino Pecci—known to all the world as Leo XIII—issued the papal encyclical *Rerum Novarum*. It too spawned a decades-long resurgence of dynamic Catholic social policy. But like Kuyper's speech, the encyclical's greatest contribution was to give impetus to the international and ecumenical *Distributist Movement*.

In 1891, the energetic and irascible Alexander Lyle Stuart—known to all the world as a Southern Confederate partisan-turned-gentleman book binder—reprinted the works of the great statesman and political theorist John C. Calhoun with a brilliant and stirring introduction that called for a return to the underlying precepts of Southern culture. Rallying around his ideas of property, family, and community, a whole new generation of

Southern intellectuals regenerated the old notions of political decentralization and overlapping spheres of social authority—and thus gave rise to the *Southern Agrarian Movement.*

In 1891, the tireless and articulate Henry Cabot Lodge—known to all the world as an esteemed senator from the state of Massachusetts and a popular historical revisionist—delivered his most famous oration, entitled *Justice as the Fruit of Christian Diligence.* Delivered in Boston before luminaries assembled in celebration of the centennial of the Bill of Rights, the speech had an immediate short-term impact, but its long-term effect was to spawn the *American Progressive Movement.*

In 1891, a Calvinist, a Catholic, a Confederate, and a Caliban suddenly united—albeit unknowingly—to stand against the rising tide of ideology, to posit an all-encompassing worldview alternative, and to affirm with one voice the essential dynamic of the unencumbered Christian social ethic—the only substantial hopes for the disenfranchised and dispossessed in this poor fallen world. Distinctly anti-revolutionary, they stood on the firm foundation of old truths, long confirmed in the experience of men and the revelation of God.

Thus, as amazing as it may seem at first glance, each of the four great men—and each of the popular Christian resistance movements they conceived—shared five essential presuppositions. Their astounding unanimity, I believe, is nothing short of a brash witness to the superintending grace of a sovereign God. Whether Christian Democrat, Distributist, Southern Agrarian, or Progressive, these five principles remained fundamental to them all.

First, they shared a profound distrust of central governments to solve the grave problems that afflicted society in general and the poor in particular. Each believed in a strong and active civil authority—but only in its proper place. Thus every brand of statist ideology was abhorred by them. Kuyper warned against the danger of "reducing the society to the state or the state to society." For the state to "take over the tasks of society and of the family therefore lies outside its jurisdiction." He also urged that Christians not grant the state more than should be allowed:

> Just as definitely, we must choose . . . which side we as Christians will take in the controversy between State and Society. He who would, like the Social Democrats, allow the state to be absorbed by society thereby denies the implanted authority which must strive to maintain His majesty and His justice. And whoever, on the contrary, would, like the State Socialists, allow society to be absorbed in the state, bears incense for the deification of the state; the state in place of God, and the free society ordained by God now destroyed for the sake of deifying the state. Against both of these, we as Christians must hold that State and Society each has its own sphere, or, if you will, its own sovereignty; and that the social question cannot be solved rightly unless you recognize this.

In harmony, Pope Leo argued, "The contention that the civil government should at its option intrude into and exercise control over the family and the household is a great and pernicious error." While Lodge insisted, "Government is but a tool. If ever we come to the place where our tools determine what jobs we can or cannot do, and by what means, then nary a fortnight shall pass in which new freedoms shall be wrested from us straightaway. Societal problems are solved by families and communities as they carefully and discriminantly use a variety of tools." They believed charity—like so much else in society—should be designed to avoid what Leo called the "interference of the state beyond its competence."

The *second* principle that the Christian Democrat, Distributist, Southern Agrarian, and Progressive movements all shared was a deep and abiding commitment to widespread private property ownership. Each believed that if the poor were to be equipped and enabled over the long haul, they must be afforded the opportunity to work toward owning their own homes, tending their own gardens, and passing on an inheritance to their own children. This precluded all forms of egalitarianism, socialism, and welfarism—as well as the smothering tax structures necessary to support them. As Pope Leo said, "If one would undertake to alleviate the condition of the poor masses, the centrality and inviolability of private property must be established and protected." Similarly, Stuart asserted that:

> Ownership of the means of production cannot be entrusted to socialistic bureaucrats any more than to monopolistic plutocrats. Three acres and a cow may seem hopelessly out of date as an answer to the cries of the needy—especially in light of the burden of taxation and regulation heaped upon the freeholds of our day. But the great lesson of history is clear enough: when men are left free to faithfully work at home, they are happiest and society is securest.

True charity, they believed, was what Kuyper called the "broadest distribution of property through legitimate work as is humanly possible."

The *third* principle that the Christian Democrat, Distributist, Southern Agrarian, and Progressive movements all shared was a healthy understanding of human anthropology. They took into account the Fall. Thus, unlike the prevailing ideologies of the twentieth century, they expected no utopia, no quick fix, no magic wand, no ultimate solutions to the problems of social justice this side of eternity. They recognized the sway that greed, avarice, prejudice, and envy held in human affairs, and thus conceded the need for private associations—guilds, unions, community organizations, fellowships, and fraternities—to maintain appropriately decentralized checks and balances. According to Lodge:

> Multiple jurisdictions and free associations are hedges against both tyranny and anarchy, against both cultural hegemony and civil disintegration. The medieval guilds were not collectivist, but through communal means they enforced the necessity of upholding interpersonal responsibility and accountability—a profound Christian necessity in light of the deleterious effects of sin on men and man.

Stuart concurred, saying, "There is a spiritual cancer at work in the world. The piracy of man's fallen nature invariably mitigates against freedom and justice. Therefore voluntary associations must needs balance us—without force of state but nonetheless with force of community—and hold us to accounts." Any successful program of charity they believed would require what Pope Leo called the "cooperation of many and diverse elements within the community."

The *fourth* principle that the Christian Democrat, Distributist, Southern Agrarian, and Progressive movements all shared was an unwavering commitment to the family. Though they believed that private property was the best means for the poor to obtain a vehicle for change, and that voluntary associations girded that vehicle about with protection and integrity, the vehicle itself, they asserted, was the family. Kuyper said, "According to the Word of God, the family is portrayed as the wonderful creation through which the rich fabric of our organic human life must spin itself out." Again he said, "The tasks of family in society lie outside government's jurisdiction. With those it is not to meddle." Pope Leo called the family "the true society." Lodge called it "the primary building block of our culture. Nay, it is itself our culture." And Stuart called it "the only means by which real and substantial change for good might truly be effected." They believed that charity must be family centered if it is to be the least bit effective.

The *fifth* principle that the Christian Democrat, Distributist, Southern Agrarian, and Progressive movements all shared was the certainty that the Church was central to any and all efforts to mete out mercy, justice, and truth. They believed that while the family was the vehicle for substantive change, it was the Church that drove that vehicle. According to Kuyper:

> Jesus set apart and sent out His church among the nations to influence society in three ways. The first and most important influence was through the ministry of the Word. . . . The church's second influence was through an organized ministry of charity. . . . Third, the church influenced society by instituting the equality of brotherhood—in contrast to differences in rank and station. . . . Indeed, as a direct consequence of Christ's appearing and the extension of His church among the nations, society has been remarkable changed.

Pope Leo said, "No practical solution of this problem will be found apart from the intervention of religion and of the Church." And again, "All the striving of men will be vain if they leave out the Church." Lodge concurred saying, "Of all the institutions ordained of God upon this earth, this one has the force of integration: the Church. We cannot hope to help the helpless apart from the Church's ministrations of grace which transform the giver, the receiver, and even the gift itself." They advocated that charity be, as Stuart said "guided, defined, managed, and provoked in, through, and by the Church."

In the end, all welfare programs may be reduced to theology, or what we think of God.

The Stumbling Block

Of all the precepts espoused by the Christian Democrat, Distributist, Southern Agrarian, and Progressive movements, it was this last one that most rankled the ire of twentieth-century ideologues. During the first half of this century, the Church had already become the spurned and neglected stepchild of the modern era. It was perceived as being moss-backed and archaic. Or awkward and irrelevant. And the Church's reputation has only diminished with time. Today, it is regarded as little more than a water boy to the game of life. Sad, but all too true.

Part of the reason for this horribly low estimation of the Church is due to the fact that the Church has always *limped* through history. Men look at the all too evident, all too apparent, sometimes even glaring, weaknesses of Christ's Bride and just assume that its lame and crippled state is ample justification for dismissing its importance. The fact is, though, the Church's limp is actually a *confirmation* of its power, relevance, and significance.

After the Fall, God told Satan that the Righteous Deliverer, Jesus Christ, would crush his head. But God also said that, in the process, the heel of the Lord would be bruised (Gen. 3:15). The limp, then, that Christ's Body displays is actually a sign of great victory, not a sign of defeat or incompetence. It is an emblem of triumph. This reality is portrayed all throughout the Bible.

Whenever the Church limps through history, as believers we need not be frustrated or discouraged. On the contrary, we should be encouraged that God's Word is sure and true. For victory has, indeed, already been won. The reality is that whatever the Church does—or doesn't do—directly affects the course of civilization. It determines the flow of historical events (Rev. 5–6).

The Church has the keys to the Kingdom (Mt. 16:19). It has the power to bind and loose (Mt. 18:18). It has the authority to prevail over the very gates of Hell (Mt. 16:18). It is, thus, the Church—not governments or ideologies or systems or causes—that will determine our destiny and the destiny of our world.

The reason for this is three-fold:

First, it is the Church that offers us the source of life. It offers the Waters of Life (Rev. 22:17), the Bread of Life (Jn. 6:31, 1 Cor. 11:24), and the Word of Life (1 Jn. 1:1). The sacramental ministry of the Church is our *only* source for these grace provisions. There is nowhere else that we can turn for these "medicines of immortality." They effect a tangible offering to God, a consecration *before* God, a communion *with* God, and a transformation *in* God. Thus, they actually readjust us to the ultimate reality.

Second, the Church offers us accountability and discipline. Sin cripples any work. Whenever sin is casually tolerated, all our efforts are defiled (1 Cor. 5:6–13), evangelism is stifled (1 Cor. 5:1–5), and victory is denied (Josh. 7:1–15). Only the Church has the authority to discipline heinous sin (Mt. 18:15–20). The purpose of this kind of accountability is, of course, protective and restorative, not defensive or punitive. It is to erect a hedge of responsibility and respectability around our efforts to confront evil in this poor fallen world.

Third, the Church offers us a place of rest. When, as God's people, we assemble ourselves together, we are at last able to lie down in green pastures, beside still water (Ps. 23:2). As we gather around the throne of grace, we are at last able to take refuge and find sanctuary (Ps. 61:1–4). We are able to enter His gates with thanksgiving and His courts with praise (Ps. 100:4). In other words, in the Church, we are able to find rest (Heb. 4:1–13), restoration (Ps. 19:7), reconciliation (Ps. 32:3–6), and recompense (Ps. 73:15–24).

Without the context of the Church, even the most dynamic Christian character is exposed to atrophy and entropy. But, within that context, our witness becomes our most powerful weapon in the preordained spiritual warfare of our day—even as we limp along the battlefield of this culture. Kuyper enunciated the critical place for the Church:

> It is noteworthy how this organization was instituted so as not only to seek the eternal welfare of its followers, but also very definitely to remove social injustices. Exactly because of its divine simplicity, this organization brought forth a double fruit. From this it already follows that the Church forsakes its principle when it is only concerned with heaven and does not relieve earthly need, and it also follows that our diaconates will have to function very differently if they would truly honor Christ.

Conclusion

A lack of confidence in the state, a reliance on private property, a realistic anthropology, a reliance upon the family, and a subsuming trust in the Church: these five principles drove—and to whatever degree they still exist, still drive—the Christian Democrat, Distributist, Southern Agrarian, and Progressive movements. They represented the only serious dissent from the failed ideologies of the twentieth century. Together they comprised an altogether alternate sociology—one that was repudiated by the powers and principalities but not by providence. In fact, together they were, "a perpetually defeated thing which survives all its conquerors." So said the great Distributist, G. K. Chesterton.

In the end, we must say, along with Titus and the Apostle Paul, "These things are good and profitable for all men" (Titus 3:8). If we are to build models of Christian compassion, it will not be sufficient to merely accommodate mercy to the ideological structures of our time. We must offer a sociology of resistance like unto those birthed a century ago—a sociology rooted in the faith which was "once for all delivered unto the saints."

10. WELFARE AND MEDICAL CARE

F. Edward Payne, M. D.

In this short chapter, medical doctor and ethicist, Dr. F. Edward Payne, author of the recent Biblical Healing for Modern Medicine *and other works on bio-medical ethics, reflects on how welfare and medical care are inter-related. Both stem from the same problems, and likely find their solution in the same principles. Payne calls on us to re-emphasize the providence of God and personal responsibility in any models—either for medical care or welfare reform. Without the essential ingredients mentioned by Dr. Payne, compassion and mercy will be unrealized.*

One of the greatest detriments to the Christian view of charity is the notion of human rights. The notion of "rights" is not a Biblical idea. It is a legacy of the European Enlightenment. The notion of rights has been helpful in forming liberal societies, that is, societies formed without reference to God. No one need feel grateful or to say "thank you" in a society of rights. We are born with rights. . . . Rights promise a world in which no one will ever be indebted to anyone or have a claim on anyone, other than that of giving the other person his or her due. In short, rights enable us to create a society of strangers.[1]

A nd a woman was there who had been subject to bleeding for twelve years. She had suffered a great deal under the care of many doctors and had spent all she had, yet instead of getting better she grew worse. When she heard about Jesus, she came up behind him in the crowd and touched his cloak, because she thought, 'If I just touch his clothes, I will be healed.' Immediately her bleeding stopped and she felt in her body that she was freed from her suffering" (Mark 5:25–29).

This woman's desperation came from the same physicians whom she had visited for help! When she began to see them, she had only one problem, her hemorrhage. After "many things from many physicians," however, she had the additional problem that "she had spent all that she had."

Today, much the same scenario occurs. Patients have been to see "many physicians," and spent a great deal of money. Yet, their condition has not improved and may have gotten worse. They may have even "suffered" from these physicians. Obvious and similar parallels between this losing proposition in medicine and the ill effects of recent welfare will be made below. In fact, it will be suggested below that the systematic failures in medicine are closely related to the systematic failures of modern welfare, both having their root in a non-Biblical world view and misshapen ideas of responsibility—personal and civic.

The cost of medical care has become one of the dominant concerns of American society and recent presidential elections. With Americans paying almost one trillion dollars and 13 percent of the Gross National Product for medical care, it is not only a social concern but a gigantic business and economic concern. The cost of medical care is not only unaffordable by 37 million Americans (a bandied number), its cost for individuals, families, and businesses is also a "big ticket" item. For example, the cost of medical provisions to automobile workers contributes $1000 to the cost of every new car that rolls off the assembly line. Does this help the poor?

Among Christians, no greater confusion about medicine exists than over the application of Biblical economics to medicine. There is always difficulty separating "what is" from "what ought to be." Thus, the existing structure of medical payment for the past 30 years has inculcated the notion that its methods are "rights" and "oughts," a dynamic not dissimilar from welfarism in the same time period.

Christians with the light of God's revelation should be able to discern this issue. However, there are five major hurdles that stand in the way to this discernment. One is the lack of efficacy of medicine. That is, much—if not most—medical care does little to effect patients' health for the better. Often, harm is caused. Thus, the benefits of massive expenditures for medical care are really quite small. Another hurdle is the present structure of insurance.

Three other hurdles are charity versus government provision of medical care, the right to medical care, and the relationship of morality to health. This essay will briefly concentrate on these obstacles.

Charity vs. Government Provision

The call for Christians to be charitable toward the less fortunate is clear. In fact, a renewed understanding of real Biblical charity would be most beneficial toward solving some of these issues. One illustration of God's judgment focuses on acts of charity: food for the hungry, drink for the thirsty, clothes for the naked, housing for the stranger, and visitation for the sick and imprisoned (Mt. 26:31–46). The Apostle James makes the searing statement that our faith (salvation) is questionable if our charity is lacking (Jas. 2:14–26). Charity is to be extended even to those hated (Lk. 10:25–37), as well as to one's enemies (Mt. 5:43–48).

Perhaps, it is this strong and vividly illustrated call of God that confuses Christians in the provision of medical care for the "unfortunate." "If the government does not provide for them, who will?," is the typical question when asked if such provision is a proper role for the government. "The Church obviously will not and cannot provide the extent of medical coverage needed for these people. Someone has to, and only the government has the resources or money." Unfortunately, both in modern medicine and modern welfare, this dire confusion has surfaced.

Two serious mistakes, however, have been made in such reasoning. First, government programs have been equated with charity. Note that the Bible passages identified above call for *individual* charity, not government programs. Other texts (1 Tim. 5:3–16 for example) call for charity from the Church. The reason is simple. *Charity, by definition, is voluntary. Payment of taxes (to give to the "unfortunate") is not voluntary.* Neither the individual nor the Church has any control over how the money is spent once taxes are paid.

Second, nowhere does the Bible give the State the role of charity. Gary DeMar has defined six Biblical roles for government, but charity or welfare is not one of them.[2] One might offer an "argument from silence." That is, whatever the Bible does not explicitly or implicitly prohibit is permissible. Since the role of government to provide welfare is not prohibited by the Bible, this role is permissible.

The deficiency of this argument, however, is based in God's explicit assignment of charity to individuals and churches. It is stretching the imagination that He would permit government funding of welfare by His silence when His explicit call is otherwise. That method of design is comparable to the game, "Guess What I Am Thinking." More specifically, revelation would not be necessary. On this basis, mankind should be able to solve its own problems without any direction from God. Surely, no Biblical Christian would make that argument!

Thus, proponents who claim that God has given a role to the government as a charitable institution have no support either from the Bible or from any definition of charity as a voluntary and directed gift. As to who provides for the "medically needy," other principles must be covered before that question is answered.

The Right to Medical Care

John Warwick Montgomery has written a helpful book on the Biblical concept of rights.[3] While he does not address the subject of medical care as a right, he does establish general principles that can be applied to medical care or medical obligations under a welfare system.

First, a demand for a right is always an appeal to authority for justice. It may be an informal appeal, as I appeal to my neighbor that his 100-decibel music has violated my right to my own tranquility. Or, it may be a formal or legal appeal to a government power—bureaucrat, politician, or judge—to enforce my right, as in a dispute over a property line with a neighbor.

In essence, then, a right is an appeal to an authority. Informally, it tries to invoke the conscience of another. Formally or legally, it invokes the power of the government to force a person to behave according to some standard.

For Christians, rights exist in two areas: the spiritual and the civil. In the spiritual, the ultimate power of the church is excommunication (Mt. 18:15–20). That is, a person loses the fellowship of other Christians (1 Cor. 5:9–13) and may not partake of the Lord's Supper (1 Cor. 11:27–34). At a lesser level, church leaders settle questions of rights between believers (1 Cor. 6:1–11). The Church has no Biblical sanction for the physical enforcement of rights.

In the civil realm, the ultimate power of government is death (Rom. 13:4). Lesser penalties are fines, restitution, and imprisonment.[4]

The most important point is that the right to anything in the civil realm is ultimately backed by the power of the State with confiscation of life, liberty, or property. Therefore, the argument that medical care is a right or a part of obligatory welfare entitlements is inevitably an argument for the government to use whatever force is necessary to protect and enforce that right!

Many Christians have confused informal rights with legal rights. People in need have every right to appeal to the conscience of others to help them. As we have seen, one graphic illustration of Judgment Day involves individuals' responses to such appeals (Mt. 25:31–46). However, *the informal right to appeal is not the legal right to enforce.*

Consider the ultimate use of force in the issues of the "right to life" and the "right to medical care." Should the full force of the state—confiscation of property, limitation of freedom, and ultimately death—be invoked to protect the right to life of the unborn (of criminal action)? The answer is a resounding, "Yes!"

Now, should the full force of the state—confiscation of property, limitation of freedom, and ultimately death—be invoked to protect a welfare right in general, or the right to medical care in particular? The answer is a resounding, "No!"

Think carefully on a purely pragmatic level. Is the right to medical care so great that others' rights are not only ignored, but seized and controlled that such right may be guaranteed? *Is the right to medical care greater than all the rights of others?* What about welfare? Again, "No!"

History supports this position against medical care as a right. Welfare reformers should also call into question the view which maintains welfare as a right. The current frenzy about the right to medical care is a new concept, even in secular minds. To advocate medical care as a right will hardly help welfare recipients, despite any utopian promises to the contrary. The following was printed in the prestigious *New England Journal of Medicine* only twenty years ago.

> From man's primary right—the right to his own life—derive all others, including the rights to select and pursue his own values, and to dispose of those values, once gained, without coercion. The choice of the conditions under which a physician's services are rendered belongs to the physician as a consequence of his right to support his own life.

> If medical care, which includes physician's services, is considered the right of the patient, that right should properly be protected by government law. Since the ultimate authority of all law is force of arms, the physician's professional judgment—that is, his mind—is controlled through threat of violence by the state. Force is the antithesis of mind, and man cannot survive qua man without the free use of his mind. Thus, since the concept of medical care as the right of the patient entails the use or threat of violence against physicians, that concept is anti-mind—therefore, anti-life, and therefore, immoral.[5]

Morality, Medical Care, and Caring

Morality correlates with good health. In the United States, emphasis and enforcement of rights and freedoms have greatly exceeded personal responsibility. This cultural and legal shift has contributed a great deal to the cost of medical care. There are few restrictions to applications for medical insurance other than "existing conditions" and use of tobacco products. Thus, a person may live the profligate life of his own choosing and be covered for the medical consequences of this lifestyle.

The disintegration of the family is one example. Numerous studies confirm that married men and women are more healthy than singles (never married, divorced, and widowed).[6] Those married have fewer diseases, fewer visits to physicians, fewer hospitalizations, and fewer "psychological" problems. And, their children reflect similar characteristics for good health.

Thus, those who are moral—those who marry and stay married—have considerably fewer medical costs than the immoral. However, most insurance programs and no government programs have any criteria about being married or belonging to a family. Everyone's costs are "covered," while the reality is that the medical costs of the "immoral" are several multiples of those who are "moral." In this way, immorality is subsidized by both private and government third-party programs and the costs of medical care are increased. Can this possibly help the truly needy?

The extreme of total coverage for everyone is that designed for AIDS patients. State and federal governments have severely restricted the screening that private insurance companies may perform to detect people with AIDS or who are at risk for AIDS. Further, *government programs have been designed to give added benefits and reduce eligibility for those with AIDS or at risk for AIDS.* Thus, moral citizens *both as private insurance purchasers and taxpayers* are required—"forced" because of the "rights" of some—to pay for the consequences of the immoral lifestyles that expose people to the AIDS virus.

In the previous section, the necessity of limits on medical coverage was demonstrated. One specific of that limit should be certain moral requirements. Without moral limits, the medical bill for profligacy eventually becomes unpayable. No society can afford to pay for the medical damage that gross immorality causes. The same principle holds for welfare reform. We are seeing that reality in the United States today.

Christians who believe that welfare or medical care should be provided regardless of the lifestyle of the recipient have failed to consider that God has placed restrictions on charity in specific situations. Giving is not always unconditional. The Apostle Paul instructed the Thessalonians, "If anyone will not work, neither shall he eat" (2 Thess. 3:10). It does not take much wisdom to conclude that the person who is not allowed to eat will die of starvation within a few weeks. This harsh consequence is considerably less than a restriction placed on lifestyle to be eligible for medical care.

Timothy was instructed not to give *carte blanche* to widows, but to impose certain criteria that they had to meet before the church was to provide for them (1 Tim. 5:3–16). One criterion corresponds to what has already been said here. "Younger widows" are refused with the clear implication that they are to remarry (v. 11). Oh, such an odious restriction to "modern" individuality! But, nevertheless, this restriction is placed upon a woman following a great crisis—the death of her husband.

These texts and others clearly indicate that even charity is not distributed within or without the Church apart from moral (Biblical) considerations. It is consistent, then, to expect that medical care as a form of charity ought to have restrictions, as well. If a person lives an openly immoral lifestyle—"does not work"—neither shall he be eligible for charity in the form of medical care—"neither shall he eat."

There is, however, one qualification of this principle. Christians should be charitable and always to care. Broken lives and broken bodies should be shown the love of

Christ, regardless of what caused them. These people ought to be *cared for*. However, *caring* and *medical care* ought to be separated. A profligate person should not be eligible for the full range of medical care or welfare, but the person ought to be cared for when he has exhausted his resources and has nowhere else to turn. That is, first, the person should be offered the "balm of Gilead," Jesus Christ (evangelism). Second, as he becomes unable to care for himself, Christians ought to care for him.

Mother Theresa is an example of this distinction. While she cannot provide the full range of medical care to her patients, she can and does provide personal care. In our context, we ought not to provide the full range of medical care to the immoral, but offer our personal care when they have nowhere else to turn.

Unfortunately, caring in a medical context has become acquainted with medical care in our day, just as charity has become confused with welfare. However, with the limitations of medical care and its costs, this distinction needs to be clearly made.

Medical Inflation:
Biblical Values and the Current System

Because man's resources are limited, he is forced to choose about the property that he buys—house, cars, furniture, appliances, recreational "toys," etc. It has been said that a man's checkbook reveals where his heart is. This saying is reflected in Jesus' words, "where your treasure is, there your heart will be also" (Mt. 6:21). As an objective measure of man's desires (heart), a man chooses from his limited resources. The Christian, of course, should choose in a manner consistent with other Biblical values. These include physical provisions for one's family (1 Tim. 5:8), the needs of other Christians (2 Cor. 8:1–24), and the support of missionaries (Phil. 4:14–16) and spiritual leaders (1 Tim 5:18).

Medical care is one choice among these objective values. The "right" to medical care has caused an attempt to provide full medical coverage for everyone, much as welfare has been expanded to cover the whole range of services. The glamour of modern techniques and medicine is so appealing that most people are willing to pay considerably more to have the "latest and best." In less than two decades, however, it has become apparent that *this cost was far greater than originally expected*. In fact, this cost, under the current system, exceeded the ability of individuals, businesses, and even the government to pay.

Conclusion

The medical system in the United States—and to a lesser extent in many other countries—is built upon several fallacies that have been discussed. The recognition of these fallacies is prerequisite to a Biblical approach to medical care or welfare. The current system is in shambles. Where churches and individual Christians have followed these same fallacies, they too have found medical care unaffordable.

The great enigma is why most people are willing to spend such exorbitant funds for results that are at best only minimally effective. From a spiritual perspective, the far greater cost is a failure to obey God and His Word. It is high time that Christians re-examined these issues more closely, more Biblically, and more keenly aware of the calling to be good stewards, while at the same time acting as charitable witnesses in word and in deed.

11. A NON-THEOLOGICAL POSTSCRIPT

David W. Hall

In this concluding note and application, the editor reviews which kinds of approaches to welfare have not worked. Following a few more statistical reports which document the noneffectiveness of statist approaches, a final plea for a value-based welfare model is given. In the end, we find ourselves inescapably thrust back toward a theologically-informed policy. Welfare cannot be fair, nor compassion truly loving, apart from the revealed truths and values of God.

> *In these intellectual struggles, much is at stake for the poor of the world. Ideas have consequences, especially for the poor. These days, the consequences of bad ideas are slowly leading more and more inquirers toward the rediscovery of the constitution of liberty: political liberty from torture, economic liberty from poverty, and liberty of conscience, information, and ideas . . . Nothing so lifts up the poor as the liberation of their own creative economic activities.*[1]

*I*n what has preceded, the emphasis has been on providing a uniquely Biblical rationale for welfare. The study has been unashamedly and undeniably revelation based. Notwithstanding, it is also the contention that even nonrevelation-based approaches confirm the aforementioned principles. At the conclusion of this Biblical synthesis it is interesting to note that many in our own modern welfare state are confirming the above Biblical postulates by reaching some of the same conclusions. This chapter presents a summary of current examples that documents what doesn't work, gives seed examples for what does work, and stresses that one often ignored key is to recognize the moral and theological component needed.

Programs That Didn't Work

From some of the following it can be seen just how wrong the Great Society programs from 1960–1990 were. It has been documented that in 1962 the total cash payments expended to the poor were in the ten billion dollar range and by 1990 that had barely doubled. In contrast, however, the noncash spending increased from about 16 billion, nearly ten-fold, to almost 140 billion. This shows precisely that what does not work is the distribution of welfare spending through an imperialistically expansionistic bureaucracy. As others have pointed out, it takes nearly four dollars to get a single dollar into the hands of the poor, with three of those dollars remaining in the coffers of the bureaucratic welfare system. Since the mid-70s our government has spent in excess of two hundred billion dollars per year for poverty relief. As Charles Murray notes, "After all the trillions of dollars spent on welfare from 1965 to date, 14.4 percent of our population (33.7 million persons) still live below the poverty line ($10,990 for a family of four). In 1950, 1-in-12 Americans were below the poverty line; in 1979, it was 1-in-9; today, 1-in-every-7 Americans is reported to be below the poverty line."[2]

It was recently reported that the "number of children living in poverty grew by 1.1 million to more than 11 million between 1979 and 1989 . . . 17.9 percent of children lived in poverty in 1989, up from 16 percent a decade earlier, as poverty rates rose in 33 states. The highest child poverty rates were in 10 largely rural states, with Mississippi having the highest rate of 33.5 percent."[3] All this decline was accomplished by an 18 percent increase in per capita income during the 80s, and the 27 percent increase in gross national product.[4] In response, Gary Bauer, of the Family Research Council, opined that "most of the growth is due to out-of-wedlock childbirths. No matter what the government does, if a 15-year-old has a baby that is another impoverished household. . . . In 1984, welfare expenditures accounted for some 64 percent of the Federal Budget."[5] By spring of 1992, it was reported that nearly one-in-ten Americans were on food stamps as well.

One of the prophets of the anti-welfare state was policy analyst Charles Murray. In his ground-breaking *Losing Ground* (1984), he chronicled what had not worked from 1950 to 1980. In an update in 1992, his earlier contentions—that statist welfare was not lifting many up from poverty, but rather stultifying it—had still not been falsified. Murray, contrary to much of the media and faint hearted politicians, affirmed that it was precisely the post-1960s reforms which were partially to blame for such things as the Los Angeles riots in the spring of 1992. By first faulting the transformation of social policy toward the poor and disadvantaged in the domains of welfare, education, and criminal justice, Murray analyzes:

> The new wisdom had many elements, but the most fundamental and pervasive was the shift away from a belief in America as the Land of Opportunity, with the best and fairest system in the world, benign and self-correcting, toward an assumption that the American system is deeply flawed and is responsible for the plight of the disadvantaged. Poverty, it was concluded, is caused by structural features of capitalism. If a student misbehaves in school or a young man snatches a purse or a young woman has a baby without a husband, these are expressions of or responses to social conditions beyond their control. Value judgements themselves are inappropriate. Having a baby without a husband is a choice, not a sin or even necessarily a mistake. It is society that must change, not individuals; the rich must see the error of their ways, not the poor the errors of theirs. To hold people accountable for their behavior is unjust—blaming the victim. Root causes must be corrected.[6]

Moreover, Murray speaks of the nonbeneficial effects of the permeation of these welfare reforms on blacks in particular:

> During this period, a variety of trend-lines for measuring the status of working-age blacks began to take a turn for the worse. Illegitimacy among blacks had been rising slowly; in the mid-60s, the slope of the trend-line suddenly steepened. Homicide among blacks had declined during the 50s. In the mid-60s, it shot up, along with black arrest rates for violent crime. Black marriage rates and male labor-force participation both plummeted, after a history of remaining near or above white norms.[7]

It becomes increasingly clear that the 1960–1990 generation of welfare has helped few. According to a recent study by the Joint Center for Political Studies, little optimism is expressed regarding the present welfare system:

> Like many other Americans, most blacks are skeptical about current welfare policies. Some 57 percent believe government should not increase aid when single mothers have more children, and 75 percent think such a policy change would encourage single women to have fewer children. The poll found 91 percent of blacks support opportunities for low-income people to become homeowners by buying public housing.[8]

It is still more shocking to note that "Despite a great society effort now well into its third decade—the cost of more than 2.5 trillion dollars—the life of many inner city residents has never been worse, for blacks especially. Today, blacks comprise almost half of the prison population. The homicide rate for black males age 15–24 has increased by 40 percent since the mid-1980s, and is now the leading cause of death for that age group. Forty percent of those murdered in the U.S. are black men killed by other black men. Sixty-five percent of all black babies are born to unwed mothers; the number is as high as 80 percent in many inner cities."[9]

Moreover, Richard Neuhaus editorializes that, "In the 1950s, nearly one-third of poor families were headed by adults who worked full time. That figure today is 16 percent. Even using the Census Bureau's skewed definition of poverty, only 5.6 percent of married-couple families are today 'living in poverty.' In 1959, 28 percent of poor families with children were headed by women. Today, more than 60 percent of poor families with children are headed by single mothers."[10] Further, Neuhaus reports an often overlooked, but pertinent fact: ". . . the government's own data show that low-income households spend $1.94 for every one dollar of income reported. . . . If all welfare benefits are included, the government is spending over $11,120 on every 'poor' family in America." His conclusion is that the remedy does not lie in more government programs, but more in recognizing that "the reality of the underclass has to do mainly with culture and patterns of personal behavior."

In a related comment, stemming from observations on the 1992 Los Angeles riots, it was reported that, "The Federal Government will spend $731 billion on social programs this year, 5.3 times more (in constant dollars) than in 1965. When you factor in state and local efforts, the nation now funnels over $1 trillion into social welfare, or about 19 per cent of GNP, as against 11.5 per cent back in 1965."[11] If asked "Are we better off than 30 years ago," it would be difficult to give a Reaganesque affirmative answer in regard to welfare. Moreover, as the total population rose 8 percent since 1981, "means-tested federal spending on children and families rose 18 per cent,"[12] to only decrease the poverty level 1 percent. Is the present system working?

One of the most recent and thoroughly documented studies of the failure of the 1960–1990 generation of welfare to actually help blacks is Andrew Hacker's *Two Nations: Black and White, Separate, Hostile, Unequal.* In this study,[13] which is not designed to lambast Great Society approaches, Hacker reports some of the following:

> Nearly two thirds of black babies are now born outside of wedlock, and over half of black families are headed by women. The majority of black youngsters live only with their mother; . . . in over half of these households, she has never been married. At last count, over half of all single black women have already had children, and among women in their mid- to late-thirties, less than half have intact marriages . . . three to five times greater than for white households, and markedly higher than those recorded for black Americans a generation ago.

Moreover, Hacker reports:

- From 1950 to 1990 the percentage of black households headed by women rose dramatically from 17 percent to 56 percent (a 330 percent increase in 40 years), whereas the percentage of white households headed by women rose from 5.3 percent to 17.3 percent in the same period (an increase of similar percentage). It appears from this figure that the percentage increase was comparable between races, regrettable in both cases. However, with the figures for blacks being larger to begin with, an over-threefold increase yields a much higher number of matriarchally headed homes, with households headed by women now in the majority among blacks.

- "Since 1970, black multigenerational households have increased threefold. Three-quarters of the child-mothers have never been married, and many have dropped out of school to bear and care for their babies."

- "More than half of black mothers have never been married, which works out to three times the white rate and five times what it was for their own race a generation ago."

- Among black teenagers, 68.6 percent have had intercourse by age 15 (with the same group of whites being 25.6 percent). Neither is encouraging, but blacks had three times the frequency of this immorality. Furthermore, over 40 percent of black girls have become pregnant by age 18.

- The increase in out-of-wedlock births from 1950–1988 was 16.8 percent to 63.7 percent among blacks, with 1.7 percent to 14.9 percent among whites. Again, both races have bargained for their own problems with this immorality, which is often rewarded with greater welfare subsidy. Still, however, with nearly two out of three black babies born out of wedlock, one sees a dramatic failure.

- 51.2 percent of black children do not live with a father and 56.2 percent of black families are headed by women. 35.3 percent of those mothers who head black homes have never been married, communicating a potent, and damning message to a new generation. By contrast, in 1960 only 2.1 percent of black children had mothers who'd never been married.

Evidently, some large social dynamic is in dire need of treatment. Charles Colson even goes so far as to call for "a major reform—a better word might be a counter-revolution . . . in government policy to liberate the millions we have imprisoned in the warm embrace of paternalistic government aid programs. We need to free our subsidized, permanently dependent underclass."[14]

The most recent census report shows that the percentage of American children living with both parents declined from 85 percent in 1970 to 72 percent in 1991.[15] Add to this the much-ballyhooed recent Census Bureau report on poverty, which estimates that over 30 million Americans live in poverty, and one can see the trend lines clearly. With the poverty line being drawn at just below $14,000 in cash income for a family of four in 1991, approximately 15 percent of Americans are listed as sub-poverty line. However, the 1966 rate was 14.7 percent. So, despite the fact that this poverty line figure is more like $25,000 annual income—with an additional 79 percent of non-cash benefits, such as food stamps, subsidies, etc.—still little progress has been made, even with such gargantuan expenditures.

As Robert Rector comments in T*he Wall Street Journal*,[16] despite all this spending, not only has poverty not been significantly diminished, but negative values have been inculcated, making this course a double failure, an economic and a moral failure. Says Rector,

> Clearly the living standards of low-income Americans are far higher than the official poverty report indicates. But this does not mean that the War on Poverty has succeeded. The main effect of mushrooming welfare has been to replace work and earnings with dependence. And by rewarding dysfunctional or self-destructive behavior, the welfare state has contributed to a new "behavioral poverty" exemplified by increasing illegitimacy, crime, school failure and drug abuse. The official Census figures not only misreport material poverty, they distract attention from the real tragedy of America's welfare system: million of children who grow up without fathers, adults who lack the work ethic and the dignity it provides, and entire generations robbed of real dreams and hopes for the future.[17]

A recent editorial makes the salient point: "Liberals and supply-siders alike make an important moral miscalculation. Perverse incentives will always discourage work and encourage family breakup."[18] These writers plead: "We need welfare, training, and employment policies that instill habits of hard work and perseverance, nurture the family, reinforce authority in home, school, church, and yes, law enforcement, and which include disincentives for anti-social and self-destructive behavior. If restoring economic prosperity was the politics of the Eighties, then the politics of the Nineties must involve restoring the concepts of good character and public decency."[19] Much of this accords perfectly with our Biblical study above.

These and other studies can document what does not work in terms of welfare remedies. The mere spending of federal monies in a nonmoral vacuum has been proven in our generation to be a failure in attempt. It is time to reform, with better models.

Examples of What Does Work

Once again, turning to the advice of William Bennett, he notes that in certain neighborhoods in Los Angeles if, in conjunction with efforts with police and neighborhood watch groups, the neighborhood is barricaded, and if the policing of it is partially up to its neighbors, it has been shown that "Crime within the barricaded area was down by 12 percent over the previous year; drive-by shootings were down 85 percent. And crime figures outside the zone were also down, suggesting that Operation Cul-de-sac—as it was referred to—hadn't simply pushed crime beyond the wall."[20]

Steven Moore, in "Reform Afoot," specifically commends Wisconsin Governor Tommy Thompson's learn-fare program which cuts welfare grants by 15 percent for families whose children are habitually truant from school; it also cuts benefits by 45 percent for teenage mothers who drop out of school. Another Thompson proposal makes parents of teenage fathers financially liable for child support, and still another eliminates added benefits for welfare mothers who have another child. In Ohio, a project is now underway which "Pays teenage AFDC mothers an extra $16 a month for staying in school, but docks their benefits by an equal amount for dropping out." Further, "Michigan entirely eliminated general assistance for 80,000 employable adults without children." And in California, an experiment in which benefits are reduced by 15 percent after six months to discourage long-term dependency is now underway. In 1990, "Welfare rolls rose by 9 percent nationwide and 6 percent in the mid-west, but *fell* by 2 percent in Wisconsin, employing these reforms." Steven Moore notes of states successfully experimenting in welfare reform, "They are experimenting with a wide variety of market-based policy prescriptions: privatization; supply-side tax cuts; welfare reforms that reward rather than destroy the work ethic; enterprise zones; and vouchers for education and health care."[21]

The Biblical teachings on depravity and on responsibility may be helpful in our own society's analyses of welfare reform.[22] By 1992, Congressman Vin Weber was suggesting that responsibility be engendered by limiting welfare benefits to no more than four years. (President Bill Clinton suggested that the short-term help be limited to two years.) His point was that welfare was never intended to be a permanent lifestyle support, only a temporary aid. Weber and Congresman Clay Shaw were to introduce a bill requiring welfare recipients to "spend a quarter of their time in school, training or work. After four years, cash benefits would be cut off except for those with disabilities or, in some cases children under the age of three."[23] It has further been reported that over 12 million Americans are receiving AFDC, and "about two-thirds of those on welfare at any one time are in the midst of what will be eight or more years"[24] of government subsidy. This has led several to propose versions of workfare, with almost a "pay or play" force, the Heritage Foundation even recommending that recipients do community service, like rocking crack babies.

In the same vein, the most common occurrences causing one to go on welfare—all related somehow to morality—were first, divorce and separation (45 percent); second, children born to unmarried women (30 percent); and third, the earnings of the mother fall (12 percent).[25] It is worth noting that the leading causes may all be remedied by Biblical familial and moral obedience. Accordingly, the leading cause for going off welfare (35 percent) is marriage.

Robert Woodson, President of the National Center for Neighborhood Enterprise, shouts, "Jesse Jackson doesn't get it. . . . Don't send us social programs, send us capital. . . . Despite a $2.5 trillion outlay for social services [the poor] have suffered while 70 cents of every dollar designated for programs created in their names was absorbed by the bureaucracy of the social service industry."[26]

Woodson also reports the reclaiming of a community by a Detroit church. The Twelfth Street Baptist Church in Detroit formed a company called Reach Inc. With as little as $300,000 of its assets they bought crack houses, and by virtue of that ownership, started cleaning up the community. This forced the dealers to vacate, and provided jobs for community residents as they renovated the homes. Reach Inc. then sold the properties to members of the congregation in need of housing. Through the proceeds, Reach Inc. was gradually able to purchase more of the crack houses, thus improving the property values, as well as further cleaning up the community. All on a beginning investment of $300,000. Woodson reports, "Since Reach bought its first house nine years ago, crime in the Twelfth Street community has been reduced by 37 percent. . . . Reach has gone on to establish a restaurant that is operated and staffed by community residents and which grossed $600,000 in its first year of operation. Grass-roots initiatives are transforming many of America's low-income communities into zones of safety, enterprise, and hope. Informed public policy, therefore, should embrace and support these efforts if the nation is serious about a new urban agenda."[27]

It should be remembered that even the earliest American experiments were not totally designed to reward unemployment. Even Franklin Roosevelt, in 1935, told Congress, "The federal government must, and shall, quit this business of relief. To dole out relief is to administer a narcotic, a subtle destroyer of the human spirit."[28] Harry Truman called for the cessation of soup lines and dole.[29] And in 1962, John Kennedy, the patron saint of the war on poverty opined, "Give a hand, not a handout,"[30] believing that "no lasting solution to the problem of poverty can be bought with a welfare check." As George Grant observes, in the early welfare approaches, attempts were made to include hard work, encourage responsibility, and that "Disincentives were deliberately incorporated so that unfaithfulness, irresponsibility, sloth, and graft could be kept to a minimum. From all but the disabled, industry was required."[31]

Most contemporaries interested in welfare reform may not remember life before statist domination. It may even be the case, that if not for a catastrophic event, American welfarism might not have puttered down the destructive lane it has. Historian John Willson has recently explained:

> World War II was a godsend to American liberals. The New Deal had been dead in the water since 1937, torpedoed by its fundamental failure to effect an end to depression and its increasingly annoying meddling with traditional patterns of American life. . . . A "conservative coalition" of Republicans and southern Democrats blocked almost all of President Roosevelt's initiatives at least until the foreign policy crisis of 1939–1941, brought about by the wars in Europe and the Far East.[32]

So it may be that there may even exist some historical clues as to the time of deviation from earlier forms of welfare. Could it be that earlier Americans knew what we are now having to relearn: that the state is not the Messiah, and persons and families must be responsible? It may even be time to return to some of the pre-1936 modes of welfare, most of which are revealed in the Bible.

The Moral and Theological Component

Finally, it must be noted that it is high time, in light of the fact that some of these attempts work and some do not, to note the long-ignored factor of the moral component. In these and other studies cheers are given to "responsibility" and not just to subsidy. It is important for us to learn, as William Bennett notes, "How inseparable the moral and material dimensions of the problem are."[33] As Bennett observes, "We have heard a lot in recent days about the root causes of civil disorder. Unfortunately, most of the root-cause theorists do not go deep enough; their nostrums do not address the source of much of the urban violence . . . young boys growing up in a nihilistic culture without the presence of their fathers, few positive male role models, terrible schools, and feckless churches, in other words, few civilizing influences. We should not be shocked when these boys do not grow up to be good and decent men."[34] And he concludes, "Block grants and enterprise zones cannot rebuild a shattered moral order . . . cultural problems demand cultural solutions. We will not see an end to urban despair and violence unless we attend to this hard truth."[35]

Thus, even secular analysts are beginning to note that the most promising solutions to welfare are not found in mere economic subsidy. It is not treating the outward manifestations or symptoms that will bring solutions to welfare reform, but it must be a strategy that is aimed first and foremost at the moral core of the person, the family, and the society. Stressing responsibility and proper incentives, and informed by the reality—both theological and economic—that people will not be put on their own, but instead must be encouraged by a structure, the structure of a disciplined community of faith in which Christ is Lord over the whole life.

Put succinctly, Michael Novak has urged, "Clearly, the mere supplying of the 'poverty short-fall' through monetary grants would not solve the problem of poverty, since poverty is not merely a matter of dollars only but also has a moral-cultural dimension."[36] It was also John Kennedy who exhorted at the beginning of our "war on poverty" that any welfare policy "must stress the integrity and preservation of the family unit."[37] And most recently, Lawrence Mead has commented,

> I suspect many policy analysts realize the primary needs of wayward black men are for spiritual things—direction, re-

sponsibility, and self-respect—and not for the benefits government provides. Fundamentalist churches do provide this direction best. The disordered poor are looking above all for structure. For them, the Good News has to mean order and authority before it can mean freedom. Liberal churches are too interested in liberating the poor and shifting the responsibility for their problems to the environment.[38]

Alas, it seems that even the attempt to provide a nontheological postscript on this subject fails to allow for a purely nontheological approach. Perhaps we're beginning to reaffirm the propriety of theology as an ideological basis for public policy. We simply cannot seem to avoid the religious base for social policy. Compared with an earlier day, Helmut Thielicke saw a stark contrast: "Originally—before the modern age—poverty, though interpreted in a variety of ways, was regarded essentially as an individual phenomenon, whereas in the modern age it is usually regarded as a defect in the social structure."[39] Thielicke does not advocate a piecemeal modification of the perceived defects in the system, but calls for "altering the system itself."[40] His recommendation, even though he is a theologian, should be heard in full:

The principle of the minimal state derives ultimately from the theological character of the state as an emergency order. This concept contains within itself the postulate that we should commit to the state, not everything we can, but only what we must. It is in keeping with the provisional and interim character of the state that its claims are possible only with the caveat of an ultimate 'Nevertheless.' Where this caveat is omitted, there arises the totalitarian tendency. . . . This tendency is accompanied by a similar tendency to level down all distinction, to ignore personal maturity and dignity and to degrade persons to the position of mere objects, and to establish the dominion of the per fected machinery. It was up against this background that we insisted that the state should give up as many tasks as possible and commit them to other agencies. Only thus can such spheres as education and welfare be permeated by the personal. . . . This means that the movement towards totalitarianism will be stemmed only to the degree that non-state agencies actively assume responsibility.[41]

Again, the future of welfare reform would do well to have at least a theological postscript, if not a theological foundation. To spurn Scripture is to condemn future reform to errors as great as the recent past. As Glenn Loury comments:

Our social scientists, and our politicians, have failed us. . . . The advocacy of a conception of virtuous living has vanished from American public discourse. . . . The mention of God may seem quaint, but it is clear that the behavioral problems of the ghetto (and not only there) involve spiritual issues. A man's spiritual commitments influence his understanding of his parental responsibilities. No economist can devise an incentive scheme for eliciting parental involvement in a child's development that is as effective as the motivations of conscience deriving from the parents' understanding that they are God's stewards in the lives of their children. . . . One cannot imagine effectively teaching sexual abstinence, or the eschewal of violence, without an appeal to spiritual concepts. The reports of successful efforts at reconstruction in ghetto communities invariably reveal a religious institution, or a set of devout believers, at the center of the effort. . . . To evoke the issue of spirituality is not to deny the relevance of public action.[42]

Though helpful and sobering to realize that in many respects the problems and foundational dynamics have barely changed over time, as we seek improvements in welfare the course of wisdom requires us to be reticent to

make long-standing policy which begins by defining our
challenge as one which is totally unique, abnormal, or
without prior parallel. To esteem our own exigencies as
categorically unique or a "crisis, besides being either a
by-product of inordinate fear or *hubris,* also leads to a
skewed perspective which tend to diminish rational solutions out of deference for the perceived magnitude of the
crisis." Since the time of Abraham (ca. 2,000 BC), the
following social dynamics have been present: difficulty
of labor to provide (Gen. 3:18); fratricide (Gen. 4:8);
violent homicide (Gen. 4:23); moral wickedness (Gen.
6:5 and 8:20); ecological disaster (Gen. 7–9); sexual sin
(Gen. 9:22); tribal (gang?) warfare (Gen. 9:8–9); infertil-
ity (Sarah); competition for income (Gen. 13:8–9); consequences stemming from military conquests (Gen. 14);
racial hostility (Gen. 16:12); "household principle" established, again placing the priority on familial care
(Gen. 3: 7:13; 17:9, 12, 27, etc.); homosexuality (Gen.
19:5); and family alienation (Gen. 21:8ff.)

Thus, with what sounds like the findings of causes of
poverty from a modern Presidential Commission, we will
want to be careful before ever pronouncing that we are in
a completely new or unique situation. Such claims will
have to be subjected to scrutiny, as well as to the principle enunciated by Solomon that, "There is nothing new
under the sun" (Eccl. 1:9–11; 3:15). That being the case,
the plethora of problems takes on a different cast than
when we are led to believe that we must create solutions
de novo. If the problems and dynamics are largely static,
then we are afforded a calmer opportunity to assess solutions with more reason and balance, than a hasty attempt
to create a "Great Society" without the larger principles
given by the Great Creator of society. If all is not in
crisis, we may view solutions more rationally. One of the

aspects of this approach is that both problems and helpful solutions will be normatively similar over time. The root problems and/or remedial reforms have not changed substantially. Once again, an aged set of norms may be flawed at the outset, with an unreal assessment of historical similarities.

With a Fallen universe as a constant in our formulations, resulting welfare reform will be delimited from seeking either utopian or totalitarian means and ends. As Ronald Nash comments, "No economic or political system that assumes the essential goodness of human nature or holds out the dream of a perfect earthly society can possibly be consistent with the Biblical world view." Realism about depravity must be included in any successful welfare reform.

Finally, a realism as to the continuing existence of poverty is taught in the Scriptures. Despite the tone of resignation, Solomon, in Ecclesiastics 5:8, says: "If you see the poor oppressed in a district and rights denied, do not be surprised at such things . . ." and later queries, "Do not all go to the same place? All man's efforts are for his mouth yet his appetite is never satisfied. What advantage has a wise man over a fool? What does a poor man gain by knowing how to conduct himself before others?" (Eccl. 6:6c–8). Despite the pessimism of this verse, Solomon may be in agreement with Jesus who later taught that "the poor you will always have with you." The Bible manifests a realism, a startling absence of utopianism, not expecting that all poverty will be eradicated by some program or any institution.

So yes, the Bible does speak to this issue, and it speaks volumes. Isn't it time, especially in light of the manifest failure of human systems, that we construct a welfare system based on these norms? A more compassionate practice would result. The Bible addresses this issue, and the extent of its information is quite large. Ancient solutions for modern problems may be more promising than modern solutions for ancient problems.

A survey of different states presently attempting welfare reform confirms parallels between Scripture and experience in this area. Although these vary in some specifics, nonetheless, in the main these states are approaching a surprising consensus of reform principles. The following aspects were culled from a survey of ten states presently seeking reform:

1. Parental responsibility.

2. Support of a productive work ethic.

3. Requirement of minimal ethical behavior as a precondition for benefits.

4. Economic incentive for responsible and productive behavior.

5. Welfare as short-term relief, rather than an enduring lifestyle, with specified time limits.

6. Incremental reduction of benefits as a disincentive to permanent welfare status.

7. Encouragement of further education or job training, to prevent long-term dependence.

8. Support of the family, rather than movement subsidy, as the best means for sustenance.

9. Discouragement of out-of-wedlock births, or parental irresponsibility.

10. Encouragement to exceed normal welfare economic ceilings, so as to give incentive for recipi-

ents to become productive workers in pursuit of financial self-support.

11. Disqualification of emigrating recipients from receiving higher welfare payments by moving into a state with higher monthly allowances.

12. Requirement of unmarried women to be cared for by their family, if at all possible.

13. Responsible contractual basis to receive benefits, such that if the contract is violated by recipients, the state is not necessarily obliged to continue benefits.

It is heartening to see these various states, apart from overt pleas from the Christian community, adopting principles which conform to Biblical teaching on welfare structure. From these various state proposals, we observe the preceding planks of welfare reform, which planks are compatible with the teaching of Scripture. Some of these mirror the conclusions of earlier Biblical studies (See chapters 5–6).

Christians may rejoice at this progress. And even if driven by economic realities more than theological principles, nevertheless, many of these welfare reforms are the types which Biblical Christians have been urging for some time. As nearly all of these were in their initial stages of experimentation, they bear observation. However, at this moment, Christians can be in the vanguard of leadership in this area on both moral and Biblical grounds as few other groups can.

APPENDIX:
The Oak Ridge
Affirmations and Denials

AFFIRMATIONS	DENIALS
1. We AFFIRM that there is a Biblical relationship between faith and work, word and deed. Further, we confess Christ as Lord over all realms of life.	1. We DENY that piety or spirituality exempts Christians from concerns with physical needs. Further, we deny any gnosticism which isolates the physical from the spiritual.
2. We AFFIRM that the evangelical and reformed churches have been slack in ministry to the poor in our time.	2. We DENY that our responsibility as Christians will be lessened in the coming days.
3. We AFFIRM that U.S. government programs since 1960 have squandered many resources, lifting few out of poverty.	3. We DENY that the current approach, which centralizes and expends approximately 75 percent on overhead, bears much promise for the future.
4. We AFFIRM that the present welfare system is counter-productive, ill-conceived, and substantially immoral.	4. We DENY that the present welfare system is the proper starting point for caring for the poor.
5. We AFFIRM that the Church should call prophetically for the adoption of Biblically valid systems of caring for the poor.	5. We DENY that any system of caring for the poor can be neutral either in religious principle or moral effect.
6. We AFFIRM that God has created man in His own image to be creative and productive, and that God has enabled him, under proper conditions, to produce sufficient goods for all people everywhere.	6. We DENY that there is inherent scarcity in the finite universe to thwart industry or necessitate poverty.
7. We AFFIRM that God expresses a concern for the poor in the Scriptures.	7. We DENY that God has a concern for poverty as a consequence of sin beyond other categories of sinful consequence.

AFFIRMATIONS	DENIALS
8. We AFFIRM that Scripture teaches that God blesses those, especially the poor themselves, who help the poor.	8. We DENY that Scripture approves a callous indifference to, or ignorance of, the oppression of the poor.
9. We AFFIRM that the Church is charged to be the major extra-family agency of welfare for its members and charged with the prophetic task of calling for, and modeling, justice and mercy in the world.	9. We DENY that civil government is the agency of first recourse for the amelioration of poverty.
10. We AFFIRM the Biblical priority among helping agencies (as in I Tim. 5), viz.: a. Personal responsibility b. Family support c. Local/area church d. Other voluntary organizations	10. We DENY that the Church is the first agency responsible for amelioration of the poor.
11. We AFFIRM the Bible's emphasis on industriousness and honest responsibility.	11. We DENY that free handouts and assistance have remedied poverty in our culture.
12. We AFFIRM that the Church or family shall assist only those who are willing to work or unable to work.	12. We DENY that the Church is not free to espouse its beliefs and Biblical ethics while dispensing material aid; nor that it cannot advocate certain Biblical-ethical behaviors as prerequisites for assistance.
13. We AFFIRM that Providence is a limiting factor for the total eradication of poverty.	13. We DENY that all problems can be cured by any agency prior to the eschaton (end time).
14. We AFFIRM that there are deserving poor.	14. We DENY that the undeserving poor should be given aid.
15. We AFFIRM that an active ministry of mercy is one of the marks of an obedient church.	15. We DENY that any churches are exempt from the mandate to institute and maintain ministries of mercy.
16. We AFFIRM that righteousness is a combination of justice and mercy and that all people and institutions fall short of both standards.	16. We DENY that justice is a part of charity.
17. We AFFIRM justice to mean rendering impartially to everyone his due in accordance with God's moral law.	17. We DENY that justice entails any ideal distribution of wealth in society.

AFFIRMATIONS	DENIALS
18. We AFFIRM that justice requires the remediation and vindication of those who are impoverished by the oppressive acts of others, and that this is the primary task of the State in helping the poor.	18. We DENY both that justice permits partiality to anyone in the enforcement of laws and that the poor can be expected to defend themselves adequately against oppression without help from mediating institutions and the state.
19. We AFFIRM that we should not only provide material aid for the genuine poor, but Biblical counsel and accountability as well.	19. We DENY that real charity requires us to subsidize those who persist in moral rebellion.
20. We AFFIRM that principles of Biblical economics must be included as a basis for welfare.	20. We DENY that non-Biblical principles of economics (e.g., Marxism, or unprincipled greed) will help in remedying poverty.
21. We AFFIRM that a politico-economic system that promotes human liberty, justice and productivity is crucial to the prevention and reduction of poverty.	21. We DENY that any politico-economic system apart from the Christian ethic is an adequate solution to poverty.
22. We AFFIRM the Bible as the only infallible guide to proper care for the poor.	22. We DENY that approaches which contradict Biblical wisdom can prove fruitful.
23. We AFFIRM that there are many causes of poverty.	23. We DENY that poverty or welfare can be reduced to any single variable, unless it is an explicitly Scriptural dynamic (i.e. sin).
24. We AFFIRM voluntary charity as the best replacement for statist approaches.	24. We DENY that the civil government's power to tax justifies a general system of wealth redistribution.
25. We AFFIRM that health is a condition of both body and soul (spirit) and that medical care should be practiced with that understanding.	25. We DENY that government control or provision of health care is the best means of making health care available to the needy.
26. We AFFIRM that the goal of charity is to enable its recipients to become self-supporting and able to help others.	26. We DENY that approaches which engender attitudes of dependency on the state for the long term are either helpful or moral.
27. We AFFIRM that some cases of need are systemic or enduring and will require continuing mercy.	27. We DENY that recipients of long-term mercy are incapable of productivity or meaningful ministry.

Doug Bandow, Michael Bauman, Cal Beisner, Joel Belz, Mark Buckner, Michael Cromartie, Robert Dotson, David Dunham, George Grant, David Hall, Randy Nabors, Ed Payne, Hilton Terrell
October 24, 1992

NOTES

Chapter 1—Toward a Post-statist Theological Analysis of Poverty

1. Helmut Thielicke, *Theological Ethics* (Grand Rapids, MI: Eerdmans, 1979), 2:291–92.
2. Despite promises to end "welfare as we know it," by the end of his first full year, President Clinton had not offered a reform plan to do so.
3. Michael W. Kelley, "Capitalist Morality and the Politics of Socialism," *Contra Mundum*, no. 4 (Summer 1992), 4.
4. Ibid.
5. Paul Johnson, "Whatever Happened to Socialism," *Reader's Digest*, Oct. 1991, 112.
6. R. Emmett Tyrrell, Jr., "Unheavenly Cities," *The American Spectator*, July 1992, 10.
7. Andrew M. Greeley, "A 'Radical' Dissent," *Challenge and Response: Critiques of the Catholic Bishops' Draft Letter on the U.S. Economy* (Washington, DC: Ethics and Public Policy Center, 1985), 43.
8. Marvin Olasky, "Culture of Irresponsibility?" *World*, May 23, 1992, 7. For a full treatment of this subject, concentrating primarily on the evolution of American welfare models in the past 150 years, cf. Olasky's book-length treatise *The Tragedy of American Compassion* (Wheaton, IL: Crossway, 1992).
9. Colonel Doner, *The Samaritan Strategy* (Brentwood, TN: Wolgemuth & Hyatt, 1988), 138.
10. Ibid., 140.
11. George Grant, *Bringing in the Sheaves* (Brentwood, TN: Wolgemuth and Hyatt, 1988), 14.

12. Ibid., 16.

13. Doner, *The Samaritan Strategy*, 141.

14. Ibid.

15. Ed Rubenstein, "Why the Poor Stay Poor," *National Review*, June 8, 1992, 16.

16. Doner, *The Samaritan Strategy*, 142.

17. Rubenstein, "Why the Poor Stay Poor," 16.

18. "Toward the Future," *Challenge and Response*, 22 and 20.

19. Ibid., 20.

20. Michael Novak, "Toward a Family Welfare Policy," *Gaining Ground: New Approaches to Poverty and Dependency*, ed. Michael Cromartie (Washington, DC: Ethics and Public Policy Center, 1986), 52.

21. Steven Moore, *National Review*, May 11, 1992, 36.

22. Ibid.

23. Ibid., 38.

24. Grant, *Bringing in the Sheaves*, 27.

25. Ibid., 28.

26. Ibid., 29.

27. Ibid., 33.

28. William J. Bennett, "The Moral Origins of the Urban Crisis," *Wall Street Journal*, May 8, 1992, A8.

29. Ibid.

30. Ibid.

31. Michael Novak, *Will It Liberate?* (New York: Paulist Press, 1986), 50.

32. Ronald Nash, *Poverty and Wealth* (Wheaton, IL: Crossway, 1986), 10.

33. Or as George Will commented in 1985, "The National Conference of Catholic Bishops has discovered that God subscribes to the liberal agenda," *Challenge and Response*, 68.

34. Ibid., 11.

35. Nash, *Poverty and Wealth*, 57.

36. P. T. Bauer, "Ecclesiastical Economics: Envy Legitimized," *Is Capitalism Christian?* ed. Franky Schaeffer (Wheaton, IL: Crossway, 1986), 341.

37. Greeley, "A 'Radical' Dissent," 33–34.

38. Peter L. Berger, "Can the Bishops Help the Poor?" *Challenge and Response,* 58.

39. Nash, *Poverty and Wealth,* 59.

40. William J. Bennett, *The De-Valuing of America* (New York: Summit Books, 1992), 208.

41. William H. Willimon, "The Effusiveness of Christian Charity," *Theology Today,* April 1992, 75–76.

42. See, for example, the studies by Ron Sider, *Rich Christians in an Age of Hunger* (Downers Grove, IL: Inter-Varsity Press, 1977), or by Robert Goodzwaard, *Capitalism and Progress* (Grand Rapids, MI: Wedge/Eerdmans, 1979) for redistributionist-leaning treatises. On the other hand, for more conservative studies, one could consult *Prosperity and Poverty* by E. Calvin Beisner (Wheaton, IL: Crossway, 1988), or *Bringing in the Sheaves* by George Grant (Brentwood, TN: Wolgemuth and Hyatt, 1988), or *Productive Christians in an Age of Guilt-Manipulators* by David Chilton (Tyler, TX: Institute for Christian Economics, 1986), or Ronald Nash's *Poverty and Wealth* (Wheaton, IL: Crossway, 1986) for representative studies. Also, for a fine assortment, one could consult *Is Capitalism Christian?* ed. by Franky Schaeffer (Wheaton, IL: Crossway, 1985).

Chapter 2—Real Welfare Reform: An Idea Whose Time Has Come

1. Glenn C. Loury, "God and the Ghetto," *The Wall Street Journal,* Feb. 25, 1993.

Chapter 3—What Went Wrong with Welfare: How Our Poverty Programs Injured the Poor

1. Ronald Nash, *Poverty and Wealth* (Wheaton, IL: Crossway, 1986), 20–21.

Chapter 4—Statism: Land of the Free?

1. William J. Bennett, *The De-Valuing of America* (New York: Summit Books, 1992), 198.

2. Robert Higgins, "The Growth of Government in the United States," *The Freeman,* August 1990, 3.

3. Adapted from *Tabletalk,* September 1992.

Chapter 5—Three Essential Elements of Biblical Charity: Faith, Family, and Work

1. Abraham Kuyper, *Christianity and the Class Struggle* (Grand Rapids, MI: Piet Hein Publishers, 1950).

Chapter 6—New Testament Developments: Principles into Action

1. William J. Bennett, "Quantifying America's Decline," *The Wall Street Journal,* May 15, 1993, A10.

2. Cf. Marvin Olasky, *The Tragedy of American Compassion* (Wheaton, IL: Crossway, 1992), 101ff.

3. C. E. B. Cranfield, "Diaconia in the New Testament," *Service in Christ,* 41.

4. George Grant, *Bringing in the Sheaves* (Brentwood, TN: Wolgemuth & Hyatt, 1988), 161.

5. *Challenge and Response: Critiques of the Catholic Bishops' Draft Letter on the U.S. Economy* (Washington, DC: Ethics and Public Policy Center, 1985), p. 11. Despite this legitimate affirmation, the next principle in the same document, schizophrenically prohibits: "Eligibility for public assistance should also not depend on work requirements or work tests."

6. Ronald Nash, *Poverty and Wealth* (Wheaton, IL: Crossway, 1986), 181.

7. Ibid., 181–82.

8. *The Works of John Knox,* vol. II, ed. David Laing (Edinburgh, 1966), 199.

9. Grant, *Bringing in the Sheaves,* 50.

10. Ibid., 109.

11. Frederick Herzog, "Diakonia in Modern Times, Eighteenth–Twentieth Centuries," *Service in Christ* (London: Epworth Press, 1966), 147.

Chapter 7—Poverty: A Problem in Need of Definition

1. George Grant, *In the Shadow of Plenty* (Nashville, TN: Thomas Nelson, 1986) 55.

2. Michael Novak, *Will It Liberate?* (New York: Paulist Press, 1986), 125.

3. Joe Remenyi, *Where Credit Is Due: Income-Generating Programmes for the Poor in Developing Countries* (London: Intermediate Technology Publications, 1991).

4. Joe Remenyi, *Income Generation by the Poor: A Study of Credit-Based Income and Employment Generation Programs in Developing Countries* (Paper prepared for the Oxford Conference on Christian Faith and Economics, St. Hugh's College, Oxford), January 4–10, 1990, 12.

5. Rector, "Requiem for the War on Poverty," *Policy Review* (Summer 1992), 40.

6. J. Hill, "An Analysis of the Market Economy," *Transformation*, 3/4. Hill points out in the same article that "in the United States, from 1790–1980, the bottom 20 percent of the income distribution (that is, those ordinarily considered poor) raised their real standard of living by 750 percent. This was because of substantial economic growth rather than because of income distribution programmes."

7. Peter T. Bauer, *Reality and Rhetoric: Studies in the Economics of Development* (Cambridge, MA: Harvard University Press, 1984), 176 n. 5. Bauer cites an important study by D. Usher, *The Price Mechanism and the Meaning of National Income Statistics* (Oxford: Oxford University Press, 1968).

8. For example, The World Bank cautions in notes to Table 30 of its *World Development Report 1989*: "In many countries the collection of income distribution data is not systematically organized or integrated with the official statistical system. The data are derived from surveys designed for other purposes, most often consumer expenditure surveys, that also collect some information on income. These surveys use a variety of income concepts and sample designs and in many cases their geographic coverage is too limited to provide reliable nationwide estimates of income distribution. Therefore, while the estimates shown are considered

the best available, they do not avoid all these problems and should be interpreted with extreme caution.

"The scope of the indicator is similarly limited. Because households vary in size, a distribution in which households are ranked according to per capita household income, rather than according to total household income, is superior for many purposes. The distinction is important because households with low per capita incomes frequently are large households, whose total income may be high, while conversely many households with low household incomes may be small households with high per capita incomes. Information on the distribution of per capita household income exists for only a few countries and is infrequently updated." The World Bank, *World Development Report 1989* (New York and Oxford: Oxford University Press, 1989), 246.

9. Jean L. McKechnie et al., eds., *Webster's New Twentieth Century Dictionary of the English Language,* 2nd ed. (New York: Collins and World, 1977), 1400, 1411.

10. Theodore Caplow, "Poverty," *Encyclopedia Britannica* (1969 ed.), 18:392.

11. William White Whitney et al., eds., *The Century Dictionary: An Encyclopedic Lexicon of the English Language,* 6 vols. (New York: The Century Co., 1890), 4:4660.

12. Daryl S. Borgquist, *Toward a Biblical Theology of the Poor*, thesis for Master of Theological Studies, Talbot Theological Seminary, 1983. The Bible also uses words for *poor* and *poverty* that address not one's economic status (whether he has enough food and adequate clothing and shelter to survive) but one's social or political status: i.e., whether he is subject to unredressed oppression by those more powerful than he. It is unfortunate that many English versions of the Bible use the word *poor* to translate the terms used in this latter sense, since *poor* in English doesn't typically carry that sense. *Weak* or even *oppressed* would be a better translation.

13. A. T. Robertson, *Word Pictures in the New Testament,* 6 vols. (Nashville, TN: Broadman, 1931), 4:249.

14. "From Xen[ophon] onwards *penes* refers to the man who cannot live from his property, but has to work with his hands. Hence the *penes* is not like the *ptchós,* who is poor enough to be a beggar and needs help. He is only relatively poor; the opposite of *penes* is

ploúsios, wealthy." (L. Coenen, *penes*, sub-article to "Poor," ed. Colin Brown, *The New International Dictionary of New Testament Theology*, 3 vols. [Grand Rapids, MI: Zondervan, 1979], 2:820.) "A far deeper depth of destitution is implied in [*ptcheía*] than in [*pénia*]. . . . The [*penes*] may be so poor that he earns his bread by daily labor; but the [*ptchós*] is so poor that he only obtains his living by begging. . . . The [*penes*] has nothing superfluous, the [*ptchós*] nothing at all. . . ." (R. C. Trench, *New Testament Synonyms* [Grand Rapids, MI: Eerdmans, (1880) 1976 rpt.], 129, cf. 128–130.) *Ptchós* ". . . signifies utter dependence on society." (H. H. Esser, *ptchós*, sub-article to "Poor," ed. Colin Brown, *New International Dictionary of New Testament Theology*, 2:821.)

15. This does not mean that charitable giving is *forbidden* to anyone but the *ptchós*. It may be given to others to support a particular ministry or simply out of spontaneous kindness.

16. Marvin Olasky, *The Tragedy of American Compassion* (Wheaton, IL: Crossway Books, 1992). See also Marvin Olasky, "Beyond the Stingy Welfare State," *Stewardship Journal*, 1:1 (Winter 1991), 41–54.

17. See E. Calvin Beisner, *Prosperity and Poverty: The Compassionate Use of Resources in a World of Scarcity* (Westchester, IL: Crossway Books, 1988), 200–203. The figure of a real (i.e., Biblically defined) poverty rate being 10 percent of the officially estimated (relatively defined) poverty rate itself probably exaggerates the number of the poor by about 1,000 percent, as I show in my study (201).

18. U.S. Bureau of the Census, *Statistical Abstract of the United States: 1991*, 111th ed. (Washington: U.S. Government Printing Office, 1991), 462, Table 745.

19. Even that impression is, however, not accurate, as I point out in another part of my discussion. See Beisner, *Prosperity and Poverty*, 202.

20. Walter Williams, *The State Against Blacks* (New York: McGraw-Hill, 1982), 49.

21. See Olasky, *The Tragedy of American Compassion*.

22. See Beisner, *Prosperity and Poverty*, chapters 4–5.

23. Two qualifiers are necessary here. (1) "Income" must include both cash and noncash and both earned and unearned income. (2) Income, in this sense, necessary for subsistence will differ considerably depending on one's situation. A young child in a

household needs very little income to subsist; a single adult needs considerably more. A family in the tropics will need little housing, while one in the temperate zone will need more, and so on.

Chapter 8—Earlier Paradigms for Welfare Reform: The Reformation Period

1. Elsie A. McKee, *Diakonia in the Classical Reformed Tradition and Today* (Grand Rapids, MI: Eerdmans, 1988), 119.

2. Jeannine Olson, *Calvin and Social Welfare: Deacons and the Bourse Francais* (Selinsgrove, PA: Susquehanna Univ. Press, 1989). Page references in parentheses are to this work, until otherwise footnoted.

3. The term "humanist" in this study denotes the intellectual movement of the late Renaissance, which focused on a reasoned approach to issues, using the best of human thought. It was a distinct movement of its time, led for example by Erasmus and others. Luther, Calvin, and most of the other Protestant Reformers were part of this movement. Hence it is not pejorative and is not to be associated with modern humanism in America.

4. *Calvin Theological Treatises,* ed. J. K. S. Reid (Philadelphia: Westminster, 1954), 64.

5. Ibid., 65.

6. Ibid., 66.

7. Geoffrey Bromiley, "The English Reformers and Diaconate," *Service in Christ:* 113.

8. Cf. David W. Hall and Joseph H. Hall, *Paradigms in Polity* (Grand Rapids: Eerdmans, forthcoming).

9. *Calvin's Commentaries,* reprinted by Baker Book House (Grand Rapids, 1979), vol. xxi, 355.

10. *Calvin's Commentaries,* vol. vi. 328–29.

11. McKee, *Diakonia,* xi.

12. Ibid., 54.

13. Elsie Anne McKee, *John Calvin on the Diaconate and Liturgical Almsgiving* (Geneva: Librarie Droz, 1984). The page references in parentheses for the next three pages are to this work.

14. Robert M. Kingdon, *Geneva and the Consolidation of the French Protestant Movement, 1564–1572* (Madison, WI: Univ. of Wisconsin Press, 1967), 56.

15. Basil Hall, "Diaconia in Martin Butzer" *Service in Christ*, 94.

16. Ibid., 99.

17. Ibid.

18. Cf. Hall and Hall, *Paradigms in Polity*, chapter 18 for a modern translation of this and other portions.

19. Bromiley, "The English Reformers and the Diaconate," 113.

20. James Atkinson, "Diaconia at the Time of the Reformation," *Service to Christ*, 84.

21. Ibid., 86.

22. Ibid.

23. The references in parentheses in the next section on Luther's model are taken from Jeannine Olson's *Calvin and Social Welfare: Deacons and the Bourse Francaise*.

24. Atkinson, "Diaconia," 81.

25. B. J. Kidd, *Documents Illustrating the Continental Reformation* (Oxford: Clarendon Press, 1911), 230–33.

26. Bromiley, "The English Reformers," 112.

27. Atkinson, "Diaconia," 87.

28. Ibid., 87–88.

29. Ibid., 88.

30. Cf. Abel Athouguia Alves, "The Christian Social Organism and Social Welfare: The Case of Vives, Calvin, and Loyola," *Sixteenth Century Journal*, XX, no. 1 (1989), 3–21.

31. Ibid., 8.

32. Ibid.

33. Ibid., 14.

34. Ibid., 15.

35. Michael Novak, *Gaining Ground* (Washington, DC: Ethics and Public Policy Center, 1986), 65.

36. Alves, "The Christian Social Organism," 12–13.

37. Ibid., 12.

38. Ibid., 13.

39. Ibid., 13.

40. Ibid., 15.

41. Ibid., 7.

42. Ibid., 7.

Chapter 9—Against the Tide: Four Alternative Movements

1. Abraham Kuyper, *Christianity and the Class Struggle* (Grand Rapids, MI: Piet Hein Publishers, 1950).

Chapter 10—Welfare and Medical Care

1. William Willimon, "The Effusiveness of Charity" *Theology Today*, April 1992, 79–80.
2. Gary DeMar, *Ruler of the Nations: Principles for Government* (Ft. Worth: Dominion Press, 1987), 76–81.
3. John Warwick Montgomery, *Human Rights and Human Dignity* (Grand Rapids: Zondervan Publishing Company, 1986).
4. This statement is not an endorsement of the current penal system in the United States. However, a Biblical approach to civil punishment is beyond our focus here. I have only pointed out what penalties are imposed today.
5. Robert M. Sade, "Medical Care as a Right: A Refutation," *The New England Journal of Medicine*, December 2, 1971, 1288–92.
6. Bryce J. Christensen, "Critically Ill: The Family and Health Care," *The Family in America*, May 1992, 1–8. Published by the Rockford Institute, P.O. Box 416, Mount Morris, IL 61054.

Chapter 11—A Non-Theological Postscript

1. Michael Novak, *Challenge and Response* (Washington, DC: Ethics and Public Policy Center, 1985), 217.
2. Colonel Doner, *The Samaritan Strategy* (Wheaton, IL: Crossway, 1988), 138.
3. *The Wall Street Journal*, July 8, 1992, A4.
4. Ibid.
5. Ibid.
6. Charles Murray, "The Legacy of the 60's," *Commentary*, July 1992, 23.
7. Ibid., 24.
8. *The Wall Street Journal*, Aug. 5, 1992, A10.
9. Ibid.
10. Cf. the April 1992 issue of *First Things*.

11. Cf. *National Review*, May 25, 1992, 10–11.

12. Ibid., 10.

13. (Scribner's, New York, 1992), pp. 67, 68, 72, 74, 76, 231. For a less ideologically biased study than Hacker's, one could consult the 1992 updates on similar categories given by Charles Murray in *Commentary*, July 1992, 26–28.

14. Charles Colson and Jack Eckerd, *Why America Doesn't Work* (Dallas: Word, 1991), 82.

15. Prodigy, July 17, 1992.

16. *The Wall Street Journal*, Sept. 3, 1992.

17. Ibid.

18. Ibid.

19. Ibid.

20. William Bennett, *The Wall Street Journal*, May 8, 1992, A8.

21. Steven Moore, "Reform Afoot," *National Review*, May 11, 1992, 36, 38.

22. Doner, 146–57, in *The Samaritan Strategy* has a helpful section on positive remedies for welfare and what does work.

23. *The Wall Street Journal*, June 17, 1992, A18.

24. Ibid.

25. Source: House Ways and Means Committee graph, Ibid.

26. Robert Woodson, *The Wall Street Journal*, June 3, 1992, A14.

27. Ibid.

28. George Grant, *Bringing in the Sheaves*, (Brentwood, TN: Wolgemuth & Hyatt, 1988), 30.

29. Ibid.

30. Ibid.

31. Ibid., 31.

32. John Willson, "World War II: The Great Liberal War" *Imprimis*, May 1992, vol. 21, no. 5, 1. Another fine study, *America in the Great War: The Rise of the War Welfare State* by Ronald Schaffer (New York: Oxford Univ. Press, 1991), supports the notion that statist welfare programs were only tolerated in the early twentieth century under the guise of emergency measures.

33. Bennett, *The Wall Street Journal*, May 8, 1992.

34. Ibid.

35. Ibid.

36. Michael Novak, "Toward a Family Welfare Policy," *Gaining Ground* (Washington, DC: Ethics and Public Polity Center, 1986), 56.
37. Ibid., 57.
38. Lawrence Mead, *Policy Review* (Fall 1992), 91.
39. Helmut Thielicke, *Theological Ethics* (Grand Rapids, MI: Eerdmans, 1979), 296.
40. Ibid., 297.
41. Ibid., 316.
42. *The Wall Street Journal,* Feb. 25, 1993.

AUTHOR BIOGRAPHIES

DR. RICHARD JOHN NEUHAUS is the Director of *Religion and Public Life*, a research and education institute based in New York. He also serves as Editor of *First Things* and Religion Editor for *National Review*. Dr. Neuhaus is the prolific author of many books, including *The Naked Public Square, Freedom in Ministry, The Good Life, Eugenics and the New Medicine*, and his recent *Doing Well and Doing Good*. Father Neuhaus is recognized by many as the leading expert on the interaction of religion and public policy issues.

DAVID W. HALL is Senior Pastor of Covenant Presbyterian Church in Oak Ridge, Tennessee. He was the organizer for the 1992 Conference, *The Church and Welfare: Providence, Responsibility Justice, and Charity*, a symposium from which this book was developed. He has also served as contributing editor to various periodicals, as well as a contributor to numerous theological journals. Pastor Hall is the author of *Windows on Westminster*, (co-author of) *Paradigms in Polity*, and *The Westminster Assembly: A Guide to Basic Bibliography*.

DOUG BANDOW is a Senior Fellow at the Cato Institute, a Washington, DC think-tank. A graduate of Stanford Law School, he previously served as a Special Assistant to President Reagan. Mr. Bandow is the author of several books, including *The Politics of Plunder: Mis-*

government in Washington, Beyond Good Intentions: A Biblical View of Politics, and *Human Resources and Defense Manpower,* as well as numerous articles and essays. An award-winning writer, he also serves as a nationally syndicated columnist with Copley News Service as well as a regular contributor to the *Conservative Chronicle.*

DR. MICHAEL BAUMAN is currently Associate Professor of Theology and Culture at Hillsdale College where he also serves as the Director of the Christian Studies Program. Formerly an editorial assistant at *Newsweek,* he also serves as the book review editor of *The Journal of the Evangelical Theological Society.* He also previously taught at Northeastern Bible College and Fordham University. Dr. Bauman is the author of several books, including *Roundtable: Conversations with European Theologians, Milton's Arianism, Pilgrim Theology,* and *Man and Marxism: Religion and the Communist Retreat.*

DR. R C. SPROUL is the founder and President of Ligonier Ministries, as well as a highly popular speaker and writer. He is a graduate of Pittsburgh Theological Seminary and the Free University of Amsterdam. In addition to his responsibilities at Ligonier, he serves as a Professor of Theology at Reformed Theological Seminary in Orlando, Florida. Dr. Sproul is the author of many books, among them *The Holiness of God, Chosen by God,* and *Essential Truths.* In addition to his writing and lecturing, he also is featured in numerous video and audio study courses produced by Ligonier.

R. C. SPROUL, JR. is a graduate of Reformed Theological Seminary and currently serves as Editor of *Table Talk,* the daily devotional guide published by Ligonier

Ministries (400 Technology Park, Suite 150, Lake Mary, FL 32746). His book *Dollars Signs of the Times* is scheduled for release in mid-1994. Mr. Sproul is currently working on a study on the life of Robert E. Lee.

GEORGE GRANT is the author of more than a dozen books on politics, social issues, and history, including *The Last Crusader: The Untold Story of Christopher Columbus, Legislating Immorality: The Homosexual Movement Comes Out of the Closet,* and *Grand Illusions: The Legacy of Planned Parenthood.* His newest book, *The Family Under Siege: What the New Social Engineers Have in Mind for You and Your Children,* profiles eight influential organizations which are hostile to the Christian and pro-family agenda. His undergraduate studies in political science were conducted at the University of Houston. He has also done post-graduate studies in politics, literature, and theology. Dr. Grant currently serves as Executive Director of the Christian Worldview Institute, an educational think-tank based in middle Tennessee.

E. CALVIN BEISNER currently serves as Visiting Lecturer at Covenant College. A former newspaper editor and publisher, Mr. Beisner is a graduate of the University of Southern California. He is the author of *Prosperity and Poverty: The Compassionate Use of Resources in a World of Scarcity, Prospects for Growth: A Biblical View of Population, Resources, and the Future, Psalms of Promise,* and *God in Three Persons.* Mr. Beisner is also a frequent contributor to various journals and former editor of *Discipleship Journal.*

F. EDWARD PAYNE, M.D. is Associate Professor of Family Medicine at the Medical College of Georgia, and Founder of the Journal of Biblical Ethics in Medicine. He also serves as Editor of *Biblical Reflections on Modem Medicine* and *AIDS: Issues and Answers*. Dr. Payne is the author of *Biblical and Medical Ethics, Making Biblical Decisions, What Every Christian Should Know About the AIDS Epidemic,* and the recently published, *Biblical Healing for Modern Medicine: Choosing Life and Health or Disease and Death*.